PHD [ALTERNATIVE] CAREER CLINIC

PHD [ALTERNATIVE] CAREER CLINIC

JANE Y. CHIN, PH.D.

PHDCAREERCLINIC.COM
Los Angeles, California

ISBN: 978-0-9755072-1-6

Library of Congress Cataloging-in-Publication Data:

Chin, Jane Y.

PhD alternative career clinic / Jane Y. Chin – 3rd ed.

Table of Contents

DEAR PHD PROFESSIONAL

Within every obstacle and every challenge hides an opportunity. This opportunity is often missed by those who fixate on the enormity of the challenge and the height of the hurdle.

In our pursuit of truth, through the highest degree we can attain in a field of study we have chosen, we have already accepted an intellectual challenge requiring commitment and perseverance.

Now we find ourselves living in a time when our PhD industry speaks of the glut of PhDs graduating and the scarcity of jobs we may hold.

Every year the PhD job market bottleneck seems to close tighter, threatening to suffocate the future of the best and brightest of inquiring minds.

From this irritating reality of the PhD employment-oyster hides the potential of a pearl of wisdom: a new future for those of us who look beyond the ivory towers of academia or the familiarity of research to make a difference.

I see new possibilities for today's PhDs and tomorrow's PhDs. I believe that we can excel and thrive in alternative careers. I believe that we can create profound social impact both within the academic institutions and beyond academia.

I know that PhDs can change the world, on their own terms, in whatever career they choose.

We can do this, one PhD alternative career transition at a time.

Jane Y. Chin, PhD

1. WHAT I WISH I LEARNED
IN GRADUATE SCHOOL

This chapter covers a few valuable lessons that I'd learned on the job, and wished I'd learned in graduate school. This chapter sets a foundation for perspective-taking and skills-building assets I want to you to develop as you go through this book. Please don't skip it!

Strengthening Empathy

I define empathy as perspective-taking: Being able to stand in someone else's perspective when viewing a problem or a situation. Some people don't think empathy can be taught, just as they think interpersonal skills are difficult to teach: you either have it or you don't.

I think empathy is cultivated by diversifying one's knowledge, experience, and relationships.

Why empathy matters:

- When you demonstrate empathy, you begin to build trust.

- When you learn to see the situation from the other person's perspective, you can move from conflict to a productive resolution or solution. When you enter new industries, you appreciate why people may respond to you the way they are responding to you. This minimizes your surprise in a new situation.

- When the other person believes that you can see his point of view and is not trying to make him wrong, he is less likely to become defensive. When the other person is less defensive, he is more likely to open up and discuss with you what his true concerns or questions are.

The value of you acquiring knowledge and experience comes from a corresponding acquisition of diversity of worldviews and perspectives. This allows you to create rapport with people outside your industry or career path who may hold a different worldview or perspective.

PhDs run the risk of perspective-myopia: our knowledge, relationships, and experiences become highly niched to the subject matter for which we train as an expert. Our strength becomes a "weakness" when it comes to alternative career paths because we are exposed to the same types of colleagues, the same lines of thinking, and the same forms of experiences.

The more you will be exposed to different experiences and relationships, the more likely you will gain access to careers and jobs you may otherwise never hear about.

4 A's of Demonstrating Empathy:

- Attend to the person: pay attention to the person and be "full present" for that person. This means eye contact, no distractions like ringing phones, and no interruptions when the person is talking.

- Actively listen: listen without formulating responses or proposing solutions; paraphrase what you had heard to make sure that you've understood what was said; ask questions if you weren't clear what was being communicated.

- Affirm what you had heard: state that you value the person's opinion and show appreciation for what he has communicated. This can be as simple as saying, "Thank you for sharing your concerns with me."

- Ask questions: in addition to questions for clarifying what you weren't clear about in the communication, you can also ask questions that further explore what was being discussed. Questions should not be used as a clever way of showing the other person that he is wrong.

Empathy is a big deal whether you work as an employee or as an employer. Empathy is one of those soft skills that makes a big difference in your ability to rapidly advance in your career, gain allies and supporters, and build trust.

Practical Application: Think about a situation where you felt understood by the other person – what has that person done to show you that he knew what you were going through? How can you apply this to show an employer that you understand his perspective?

Gaining Support

Should you care about what people think of you? Yes and no.

You don't want to rest entire sense of self-worth on the opinions of others. But working in a team setting and living among people requires us to pay attention to how readily we can gain the support and approval of the right people.

Approval matters because:

- You gain affirmation of what you are doing and that others value with what you value.

- You collaborate more effectively when people coming together to support a common cause, idea, or effort that you are leading.

- You facilitate career advancement when you gain approval from those responsible for evaluating your performance and readiness for promotion (supervisors, bosses).

I used to prefer the lone-ranger approach to work. Now I see the benefit of engaging with others and how cultivating relationships has broadened my career reach and widened my scope of work.

I also recognize a dark side to "independence" may actually be an avoidance mechanism from getting close to people and fearing betrayal.

A person who is secure in himself but is not well-liked by his peers will still struggle to succeed in projects that require collective effort.

A person who is a subject matter expert may go far by relying on expertise to advance, but his ability to "scale-up" and make a broad social impact may be limited by his ability to gain the support of key people.

Approval is one of those tricky mental models that I wished graduate schools taught formal courses on, particularly the practical aspects of gaining support and discerning approval when it comes to working with peers (coworkers, colleagues) and supervisors.

Building Career Assets

Career security is like financial security: there are no guarantees. This means you have to get serious (proactive) about learning how you can manage your career, instead of hoping the job market offers you decent odds of employment.

Managing careers is a lot like managing money:

- You need to become proactive in learning how to manage your career, the way you get proactive about managing your money.

- You can learn to build a portfolio of career assets (skills, experiences, relationships) the same way you build a portfolio of financial assets (savings and investments).

- You should educate yourself on ways to grow your net "career value" (marketability as an employee), the way you have to learn the types of financial products available to you for growing your net worth.

Once upon a time, people expected to retire from the same job they worked when they started their career lives. Today, you may expect to hold many jobs within the same career and even cross different career paths over the span of your professional life. This means you have to think in terms like "career paths" and "career strategies" and begin to define yourself not with "a job" but with "career assets".

11

Your career assets may include:

- <u>Applicable skills</u>: what can you do that produces a desired result for employers or clients?

- <u>Knowledge and insight</u>: what do you know that gives employers or clients a competitive advantage?

- <u>Relationships</u>: who do you know that can solve a problem for employers or clients, or who can refer you to someone else that can solve the problem?

Once you start looking at your career assets in these categories, you can find ways of evaluating strengths and weaknesses or gaps in your existing career portfolio.

Next, you should create a list of statements that communicate your strengths in every-day language. This takes some practice especially when you may have grown used to technical jargon and academic language, but it is worthwhile and mandatory if you want to break into any non-academic career path.

For example, if you are a detail-oriented person, your career asset may be "catching mistakes other people miss". If you are a big-picture person, your career asset may be "painting the 30,000 feet-view of a problem." If you work well under pressure and high-stress situations, your career asset may be "expert at prioritizing which fires to tackle, and how to quickly put out fires when everyone is running around screaming." If you are adept at getting to the kernel of a problem, your career asset may be "able to boil down complex questions into a pertinent nutshell."

The more descriptive you can be with your skills, the more memorable you become as a job candidate.

Practical Application: Get a notepad or blank piece of paper ready and start brainstorming! Write down your current career assets. What skills, knowledge/insight, and relationships can you offer to an employer? Share your statements with a (non-academic) friend: have you clearly demonstrated your strengths and abilities in every-day language?

Preventing Burn-Out

If there is a workshop on preventing career burn-out, I'd have to repeat that workshop every year.

Burn-out is a career landmine that many people deal with, but people put a brave façade of, "I have my act together." This façade is vicious and causes people to wonder how they seemed to be the few persons who feel in constant need of an "extreme career makeover."

Career professionals experience some form of job burn-out at one time or another. When you've worked long enough, fatigue and ennui are a mild form of job burn-out and is an expected part of the professional career cycle. What is important is to recognize when the feeling of "burning-out" is a normal part of career crests and troughs, and when the situation may indicate a need for assistance or professional help.

Leading causes of career burned-out, using a "racing" analogy:

- You felt like you signed up for the wrong race.

- You ran at a pace that is not appropriate to the race.

- You felt like you were running alone.

- You ran with the wrong group of people.

- You ran with an injury or a broken ankle.

- You over-trained for the race.

Wrong race. Feeling like you are not on the right path is not the same as the expected bumps-on-the-road that we all encounter on our career journey. Instead, this is "I think I am in the wrong career and every fiber of my being is screaming at me that I am in the wrong career".

If you're already in the race, look for the most efficient transition out of your current path (an exit strategy). If you cannot see an immediate exit, your goal is to finish the race while conserving some resources to create an exit strategy.

Wrong pace: You burn out if you try to sprint your way through a marathon. Some people have the gift of pacing themselves and not piling more than what they can handle on their plates. If you do not have this gift (I don't!), you have to set arbitrary limits on the numbers of projects/tasks you accept during a given time. Managing your pace and time is important if you are in the process of creating an "exit strategy" from an academic career track.

Isolation: Being isolated leads to burn-out, and according to scientific research by Sheldon Cohen at Carnegie Mellon University, lack of social support systems leads to weakened immune systems and reduces well-being. Surround yourself with people who understand what you're going through and people who appreciate your presence in their lives. When you are doing something difficult, like breaking into alternative career paths, you need to remain connected to a social fabric of human beings who support your goals.

Wrong crowd: Just as it's harmful to be isolated, you don't want to surround yourself with hecklers and people who drag you down and trivialize your struggles and make you feel worthless. For PhD job seekers who want to exit academia, the wrong crowd is made up of people who put down your choices to leave academia, who label your choice as indicative of your status as a "lesser" scientist, and who still regard the industry as The Dark Side. The wrong crowd is anyone who drains your motivation and energy from your goals.

Injury: I had a major injury that played a big part in my burn-out – I had undiagnosed clinical depression when I was in graduate school. I am not suggesting that when you burn out you may have depression or mental health concerns. But if you find yourself having unresolved feelings of sadness and anger, and if your sleeping and eating habits have dramatically changed –there may be some underlying physical and biochemical needs that require evaluation and intervention.

Over-training: Sometimes you can push yourself too hard and not know when to say "Stop." That can lead to burn-out even if you do love what you do. One of the ways I've learned to manage this is the setting a time limit to how much I work and otherwise create arbitrary regulatory controls. At one point I was using an egg timer to limit the amount of time I spend at the computer. You don't need to take this drastic a measure, but if you tend to overwork then you need to find a way to set limits for yourself, too.

Practical Application: Think about a time when you experienced job burn-out. What are some of the reasons that caused you to feel burned out? How have you learned from this experience to prevent future burn-outs?

Think about the alternative career you are interested in. What are some of the "burn-out" risks inherent in this career or job? How will you manage these risks if you get this job?

∞

2. THE ACADEMIC BUSINESS ENTERPRISE

Now that you've decided to leap outside traditional academic career tracks, your first impulse may be to step into your adviser office and get career advice. You would expect him to listen to your concerns about future employment, be a sounding board for your career strategies, and suggest useful job leads.

Are you nodding your head because you can depend on your supervisor to help you? You are lucky. What if you have an adviser who is not enthusiastic and even less helpful?

Think about your adviser's academic job description; what his job title states, key duties expected of him, how his employer – the academic institution – evaluates his performance, and how a committee decides whether or not he is granted tenure. These are clues to why PhD students and postdoctoral fellows or "postdocs" interested in non-academic careers may meet with resistance from members of the faculty.

Getting graduate students through a PhD program is part of academic faculty's job description; helping graduates gain employment is not.

Academic institutions do not reward faculty members for helping students and postdocs land jobs *within* academia, let alone help them with employment *outside* academia. Many academic advisers may not be comfortable talking with you about career paths in which they have no direct experience. If your academic advisers haven't worked in the corporate world or started their own businesses or ever worked outside academia, then they cannot offer you much first-hand, practical advice.

Before you can make a successful break from the academic employment system, you need to understand the dynamics of academic employment relationships, and how these compare and contrast with corporate employment relationships. Start looking at academia not as institutions of higher learning, but as an educational business enterprise. We can then compare educational business enterprises with corporate business enterprises.

Human Resource Development

A company is an organizational structure of employees resembling a corporate family tree. At the top of the tree are the founders or leaders. In companies, these are the chief executive officers such as the CEO, COO, and CFO; president, vice president, and executive-leadership layers of management. In universities, these are the presidents, chancellors, and deans.

Each layer of management aims to generate the highest returns on investment for the enterprise, by the authority conferred by job title. The sustainability of an enterprise depends on the effective management of human resources: the employees. In academic businesses, you and your supervisor are employees.

Graduate students are in trainee positions, postdoctoral professionals and instructors are entry-level employees, assistant- and associate professors are members of middle management, and professors and department chairs are in upper management. Graduate students and postdocs are subordinates or direct reports to management.

Employee development describes a constellation of activities that ensure employees can and are doing their jobs, improving skills, and continuing career growth with their companies.

In corporations, managers are responsible for developing subordinates. Managers are often rewarded financially and professionally for being good mentors and coaches for employees.

On the other hand, managers in academic businesses are not responsible for developing subordinates. Not only are academic managers lacking budget for developing subordinates, they – not the business – may be responsible for paying their staff with managers' own funding. Academic managers or advisers/supervisors are responsible for procuring money to pay subordinates' salaries. Academic managers are rewarded financially and professionally for being good researchers that raise the institutions' visibility.

Before you start viewing corporate managers as more virtuous than academic managers, you should realize that neither type of managers is motivated to help you leave their system. Both types of managers face significant pressures for keeping you in the system.

Labor Cost and Intellectual Assets

Your academic manager faces pressures in keep "his" people. If you are a productive employee, he will want to keep you in the system. If you leave the system, his peers and members of upper management may view him as a failure: for not inspiring you to stay in academia. This is the romantic face of the PhD career track.

The harsh face of the PhD career track is financial. Your academic manager's grant monies are paying your salary. Losing you has a direct and negative effect to his bottom-line: he is losing a bright, productive, and cost-effective (cheap) employee.

Postdoctoral fellows and junior faculty members are a high-value group of employees who can be paid low wages for the benefit of the academic business. Hence, some postdoctoral fellows may experience the curse of "still one more project and then we can write a good paper."

Put yourself in an academic manager's position. Your research grant has a specific dollar amount, which is usually not enough. You need highly skilled people to do the research projects in this research grant, and you need to make the grant dollars stretch for as long and as far as you can stretch these dollars.

You look at the salaries you must pay research assistants or technicians and postdoctoral fellows. You may pay both groups comparable wages, but you need to pay assistants formal employment benefits. If you don't pay fair market value in total compensation including benefits, these employees can find work somewhere else.

18

On the other hand, you know that postdoctoral fellows are wholly dependent on your status as adviser and mentor. They cannot afford to lose their status as your protégé.

You can save on benefits for a postdoctoral fellow and pay as little as one-third of what you will need to pay for an assistant, because the academic market allows this business practice. Even if you have periodic turn-over and need to train new domestic and international postdoctoral fellows, this is still a good business investment and a good way to stretch research grant dollars. The fiscal realities of the academic business foster a culture where advisers routinely discourage or disparage the desire of their students and postdocs from exploring non-academic or non-research careers. This is not always personal or intentional sabotage: this is simply "good" academic business practice.

Until the academic employment climate shifts, and until the postdoctoral career identity can be established as more than a temporary training position (in Australia, for example, postdoctoral fellows are treated as career professionals instead of training positions and paid as such), you should focus on strategies and actions that can help you compete for jobs in both academic and alternative markets.

What You Can Do

Here are action items for you to complete:

Speak with academics who have worked outside academia before. They may be few and far between, but they exist. Ask them how they transitioned. Ask them why they came back. You want to get a perspective of the challenges and rewards of working outside academia before you make the leap.

Go to the university's career resource center. Read resources and career guides available to you. Make appointments for complimentary career assessments and services.

Ask whether there are alumni networks or alumni mentors that you can contact for informational interviews. Information interviews are conversations you hold with career professionals about their jobs: what they do on a typical day, what they like/dislike about their jobs, how they got their jobs.

Participate in professional associations and groups related to your interests. These may be trade or industry groups; the key is to gain exposure to people who are doing non-academic work that you are interested in. I also recommend joining associations or groups targeting specific skillsets, such as public speaking and entrepreneurship.

For example, Toastmasters International has clubs all over the world. Chambers of Commerce host events for local business owners. These can be cost-effective ways to develop your skills versus an expensive professional development program, workshop, or another degree.

Participate in online social networks for alternative PhD career professionals. Ask lots of questions to increase the odds of one of these getting answered. Share your best practices, tips, and advice, and others will be more likely to reciprocate when you ask questions. Listen for career success stories from other PhDs who are working outside academia, offer to take them to lunch so you can ask them how they did it. Your university's alumni network may be receptive to your requests for informational interviews.

Hire a professional. If you have the financial means, hire a professional career coach, mentor, or consultant who has experience with PhD career transitions and understands the types of challenges you face as a PhD. If you find individual, one-on-one coaching to be cost-prohibitive, you can look for group coaching options, which may be more affordable.

Read articles and books on non-traditional PhD career paths. Pay attention to the "how" when you read these: how did the person break into the career? What are the general reproducible approaches or strategies? If the person found the job through word-of-mouth referral, a reproducible strategy would be networking for referrals.

On the other hand, limit yourself or abstain from blogs and sites that primarily vent about the PhD job market or the usefulness of a PhD. You want to focus on what you can do, not what you can't do. You want to learn what the advantages your PhD gives you, not join in a lamentation or condescension what you had worked so hard to achieve. With the ease of access to today's social media tools and social networking websites, you can find other like-minded PhDs for advice, encouragement, and support when prospecting the career of your dreams.

∞

3. BUILD YOUR MENTAL TOUGHNESS

Winning the mental game of career transitions into alternative PhD career starts with slaying inner demons. Inner demons interfere with all aspects of your transitioning process. They show up, uninvited, when you are speaking with a recruiter about your resume. They sit with you across the table from hiring managers and whisper into your ear why you shouldn't be there at the table competing for the job.

Remodeling your mental landscape and building up mental toughness for major challenges like a career transition require you to shift the power balance of your relationships, choosing peers you hang out with, and preventing the "job search flu".

Shift the Power Balance

If you look at some adviser-postdoctoral fellow/student relationships, it's hard to believe that you are looking at two adults interacting. Instead, it often resembles parent-child relationships, where advisers are all-powerful parents, and the fellows/students are children.

Supervisors can play upon this parent-child programming to keep postdoctoral fellows and students in the nest of academia. Supervisors can perpetuate the myth that they will always hold the upper-hand in the balance of power in the other person's career. They can leverage this parent-child programming to make their postdoctoral fellows, students, and junior faculty subordinates believe that they alone hold the key to their subordinates' career viability and success.

Let's look at how young children negotiate power. Young children learn to test their independence at a very early age, as soon as they become conscious of rules and boundaries. Children will insist on doing something on their own, even if they will take twice the time it would take for an adult to do it for them. They will not care if adults are in a hurry and become late for appointments. Thus, young children may be smaller and physically weaker than adults, but they intuitively look for ways to gain power in parent-child relationships. They start by observing adults and challenge inconsistencies.

If you have a wonderful adviser who behaves as a mentor, you can skip to the list titled "Remodeling power structures in your professional relationships", or continue below to learn how you may shift power balance in future work relationships.

Start by observing how the person in charge gains and maintains power. Is it through intimidation, guilt, or positive/negative behavioral reinforcement? Is it by inflicting subordinates with self-doubt or fear? Is it with threats of discrediting or removal of funding? Does a supervisor play favorites? Does he keep people in his department suspicious of each other, thus preventing them from banding together and gaining awareness of how the power is allocated among lab relationships?

If your supervisor has established a stronghold of power where you cannot find allies within your peers, you need to establish **a nucleus of new relationships that reduces the total leverage of one person over your entire career.**

You need to develop new connections and relationships outside of your immediate work environment. You can build relationships with people in other departments and outside academia through your extracurricular activities. These extracurricular activities may become important sources of job referrals.

Whether your adviser is supportive or apathetic, your career is ultimately your personal responsibility. You are expected to take charge of your own career and not remain dependent on the recommendation, referral, or goodwill of one or two individuals; this risks your employment viability depending on the mood or circumstance of one or two people. This is also true in companies. Employees have experienced sabotage from their supervisors who want to keep their employees within their group, so supervisors give poor personal references to prevent an employee from leaving their team.

This is a good time to get comfortable with these feelings of discomfort in having to build new professional relationships. As you grow and advance as a professional, you will be frequently pushed out of your comfort zone and familiar networks, especially when you are at the leading edge of your career growth. It's when you become too comfortable and work on cruise control that you should be concerned, and keep an eye on complacence.

Remodeling power structures in your professional relationships:

- Foster new relationships that extend your reach beyond your immediate group, lab, and department.

- Increase visibility for the value you bring to a new audience (again, beyond your immediate group).

- Creating a balanced, adult-to-adult (peer-level) dynamic in your existing work relationships.

Creating balanced, adult-to-adult interaction dynamics is a subtle art. This is more about behavioral nuances than anything obvious that you can do, or say. For example, when an authority figure asks you a question, instead of answering the question right away, you can pause for a few seconds and look at him in the eye before answering the question.

New sales professionals struggle with this type of power balance all the time. This is because sales people know that everyone tends to be wary of sales people. People become guarded and defensive when approached by sales people. Sales prospects or potential customers would then create barriers to sales people and behave in ways that would shift the power balance and put sales people in a position of weaker power.

Pay attention to the signals you may be sending with a particular pace and tone of your voice. Speaking too quickly and in a high-pitched tone may give an impression of nervousness, over-eagerness, or self-consciousness. Public speakers learn to lower the pitch of their voice and slow their speaking pace to convey confidence and authority. You can use this technique to communicate confidence.

Since we're talking about power, you should realize that authority figures who engage in power-play have sensitive radars for potential compromises to power.

If you have an authority figure in your professional circle that uses power as a tool in managing relationships and "keeping people in their place", you should be cautious with the degree of visibility you are creating independent of this authority figure. If he perceives that you are threatening his power of influence, he may become defensive and he may target you for intimidation or emotional manipulation.

If you find yourself in a power struggle, don't despair or be daunted. You are developing key skills for navigating office politics in a future job.

Practical Application: How much leverage or power the authority figures in your current professional circle have over your entire career?

Rank this on a scale of 1 to 5, with 1 as "little or no power/leverage" and 5 as "complete and total power/leverage." What is your desired number?

What new relationships should you build to move toward your desired number?

Choose Peers Wisely

If you want to look at what your life may look like in a few years' time, take a look at the lives of people you spend the most time with. These can include people online and in your virtual social network as well as people in your personal and professional circles; what counts is the amount of time you spend, not whether a relationship occurs online or offline.

Who are the people who take up most of your time, focus, and attention? What are their beliefs? What values guide their lives? Do you like what you see?

If you like what you see, then you are hanging out with people you admire, people you view as role models, and peers you are drawn to because their values and beliefs resonate with yours.

If you are not enthusiastic with what you see, it is time to assess what is attracting you to those relationships. Do you still need what those relationships are offering you? Or have you grown in a different direction?

This is not a call for you to look for people with hobbies or goals similar to yours. I used to pay attention to goals that people have set for themselves and used this to decide whether I want to invest my time and attention on a connection.

I have learned that **goals alone are not an accurate gauge of compatibility: instead, how goals are achieved is a more accurate gauge.** I've met people with admirable and ambitious goals but who were the most stressed out people I've ever met. They were always chasing the next big goals at the expense of important personal relationships. Some were never satisfied with the goals they had already achieved and seemed deeply unhappy.

When I choose colleague and peers, I have learned to look at attitudes and world view; whether the person has a generally positive or negative outlook on life, whether he is mostly optimistic or pessimistic. I am not looking for a Pollyanna who only sees positive all the time; being realistic and practical is important to me. But I don't want to be around people who expect and see the worst in everyone and everything.

Practical Application: Take a piece of paper or your notebook and write out the names of 3-5 people that you spend a lot of time with.

For each person, describe his/her beliefs and attitudes about life and working with people.

Are these beliefs and attitudes similar to yours? If yes, what is the key belief or attitude that keeps you connected? If not, what is drawing you to this relationship?

Let's turn this question around: are **you** a good colleague to have? Do you have the attitude that employers are looking for?

Employers care about a job candidate's character. When employers call people listed in an applicant's references, they are looking for information that isn't packaged neatly in the applicant's resume. This is another reason why you want to choose your peers wisely, as well as create a balanced selection of supervisory and mentoring relationships, so that when you give these people's names to an employer's human resource (HR) department you can be comfortable what your references will say about you.

I have received calls from HR as part of the employers checking candidate references. These often happen in the final stretch of a candidate's race for the job, when the employer has narrowed down a selection of high potential candidates.

As a listed reference, I have been asked tough questions about the person seeking employment, like:

- What do I think are this candidate's strengths?

- What do I think are this candidate's weaknesses?

- What is this candidate's communication style?

- How well do I think this candidate works in a team setting?

- How well do I think this candidate handles conflicts?

- Can I give a specific example of a notable achievement that this candidate has done on the job?

- Can I give a specific example of a particular challenge that this candidate has faced, and how this person handled the challenge?

- Do I know why this person is looking for a new opportunity?

- Do I know why this person is leaving his or her current employment?

- What kind of management style do I think work well with this candidate's personality?

- How would I describe this candidate as an employee?

Note that I am not necessarily asked a comprehensive list of questions each and every time, but I can tell that at this point in the job competition, my reference may potentially yield new information that can work for, or against, the job seeker. I also know that my information may be limited, and whenever appropriate, I will give concrete examples that can substantiate my claims and support my endorsement of the candidate. However, not every character reference or resume reference may be able to speak to this level of detail about a job seeker, especially if the reference has not interacted with the job seeker at a significant level.

Practical Application: Look at your current resume's references. How will each of your reference answer the questions I have listed in the previous page?

If you are not sure, this is the time to find out. You can approach this sensitive conversation as part of the job seeking process you are embarking.

If you are not comfortable with how your reference may answer these questions, now is the time to build relationships that are supportive and cognizant of your strengths and weaknesses (challenges).

Let's be honest: HR is not calling to hear all the good things that the job seeker has already portrayed in the application. They are looking for potential risks and factors that can narrow the decision pool. I am not talking about serious ethical risks (although, that may very well come up if the reference offers negative information of that kind).

Instead, I'm talking about risks of "poor fit" or "suboptimal suitability to current corporate culture." I'm talking about risks of "a bad hire" who may be complainers and gossipers that can create strife within a team and destabilize cooperation.

There are people who look at life as negative and adversarial. They constantly criticize or find what was wrong with the system, but their purpose is to complain and not to look for a solution. Managers don't expect employees to never complain or criticize or find fault, but they expect an employee who brings forth a complaint to also offer at least one possible solution.

In the business world, managers and executives are keenly aware of employees who complain, criticize, and whine but do nothing to improve the system. These employees are seen as seeds to a toxic workplace, and they become serious human resource problems that drain much of management's time and energy.

Employers dread the mistake of hiring complainers and people who gossip to their companies because these people can turn others into complainers and employees who gossip. Productivity and work morale will decline as employees spend more time talking about what's wrong than doing their jobs and working on solutions that can improve the situation.

Choosing your peers wisely should extend to people in your social networking groups. Social networks are where misery loves company! You may have been in one of these groups before – maybe even now. These peers can suck your time and drain your energy. They will highlight only the negative aspects of a situation and structure their argument with a no-win approach. To complainers and whiners, the system is what's wrong.

There are indeed cases where defects are widespread, where the system needs an overhaul, and where change requires a fundamental shift in the structure of the system: the current state of postdoctoral employment in academia is a perfect example. I don't like how the postdoctoral system works and I know that changing the current state of PhD career development requires changing "supply and demand" of PhDs graduating and available jobs.

It took more than a few years to precipitate the career bottlenecks we've seen in today's PhD academic job markets. Solutions to a large scale problem need to be multi-pronged, addressing both acute problems of PhD employment (where this book and non-academic PhD career guides can play a role) as well as confronting chronic, deep-seated problems of the PhD profession, such as examination of the current tenure system and pay scales of PhD trainees play a role.

Compared to when I was a graduate student in the 1990s, today's PhD students and postdocs are becoming activists and advocates for their peers, lobbying to improve the career sustainability over the "life-span" of a PhD professional.

Complainers and whiners, on the other hand, offer no solution or take personal accountability for what they will do to improve the situation for themselves or others. Their modus operandi is to vent, to solicit others to join them in venting, and to engage in this activity at the exclusion of seeking short-term or long-term solutions.

This is no different from working in a company that has a potential to succeed, but management is allowing a few employees to destroy the morale and culture of the company. Fighting gossip siphons off creative energy from constructive participation and problem solving. The world – and the cloud (internet) – is too big to stick around with webs of negativity. What you want to realize is that what people like this are showing is disdain and contempt for others – specifically employers.

Employers have radars to detect this. Would you want to hire someone whom you suspect is looking down on you or thinks you are stupid and unenlightened? Would you pay this person salary and benefits to come and work for you, and be the face of your company and reputation?

Employers who have been around long enough will have dealt with employees like this, and they know how costly hiring mistakes can be. It is expensive to hire, even more expensive to fire a bad employee; employers do their best to avoid hiring mistakes.

Now, you may begin to feel frustrated, negative, and discouraged because of continual rejection. The job market may really be *that* bad. You may have come too close too many times and had gotten your hopes up only to have your hopes crushed to the ground when you didn't get the job offer. When this happens, you do run into the danger of becoming negative and angry. If you turn that negativity and anger toward yourself, you may become depressed. If you turn that negativity and anger toward others, you appear bitter.

If this is the case, having a support network of any kind – including an online group where you can have a safe, possibly anonymous place to share your experiences – is crucial. You can air out your anger, frustration, and fear while at the same time look for ways to move forward. This is where you need to look for groups where moderation works to allow you to get encouragement without letting the negativity grow into a trap that keeps you from moving forward.

If I see complainers becoming influential in an online discussion group and generating high frequency of un-moderated activity, I leave that group. My own online PhD discussion group is heavily moderated to prevent personal setbacks from spiraling into destructive venting.

I have deleted discussion threads that are stated so negatively that I believe the tone is deleterious to the original poster's professional image. I have even seen violations of privacy stemming from a flame-war, where a member posts a private communication from another member, in the visible discussion area. This is a serious breach of confidentiality: this person as an employee may become a liability to the company because of the example he is setting in an online forum.

Even if I understand the person's frustration or anger, I don't want inflammatory remarks in a discussion group that attract more venting instead of problem solving. We never know who may be reading a discussion thread, including recruiters and employers. Maybe you don't see an employer or a recruiter in a discussion group – but you never know if an employee is lurking and are reading everything you are posting.

Employment interviewing is an imperfect science. This is why employers will talk about using their "gut-feel" or "gut-check-" with job seekers. Employers know that people with similar attitudes or aptitudes tend to flock together. Attitude is a critical component of company culture.

This is also why companies continue to offer employees referral incentives: employees receive a bonus if a referred job candidate was hired to the company. Companies want to hire people that their people would want to work with.

Practical Application: Open up an internet browser in "Private Browse" mode and conduct an internet search on yourself. What results are showing up, associated with your name? Are you comfortable with what you see, and read, about your online presence?

This is a good time to start setting "search alerts" with your name, so you can be notified anytime when a new result show up in the search engine. Employers and recruiters are doing this as a matter of course in hiring.

Prevent Job Search Flus

You start your job search with utmost enthusiasm and motivation. You go to networking events, put on your smiling face, fill out application forms, telephone people, email contacts, day after day…

You start feeling less enthusiastic but you keep going to networking events, putting on your smiling face, filling out application forms, telephoning people, emailing contacts, day after day…

You feel no enthusiasm, you go to networking events but you force your face to smile, you fill out application forms expecting the worst. You stop calling people. Your email contacts wane…Guess what? You have the Job Search Blues, or as I call it, the "Job Search Flus" and it feels as horrible as it sounds.

You feel like you've been hit with a truck. Each rejection is a heavy brick that knocks down your self-confidence. You have to summon tremendous effort to do even the simplest task of writing a job seeking email.

When you've been hit, there is no escaping the feeling and you have to weather through it. However, there are actions you can take to make sure that your bout of "Job Search Flu" doesn't get worse.

Step 1. **Start tracking your actions.**

How many emails did you send? How many phone calls did you make? How many job listings did you read through? How many ideas came to your head when you were researching for career options?

Stop taking for granted each and every one of these actions, and start tallying down numbers.

This also serves an important purpose: this gives you a way to measure and gauge what you produce and accomplish within a unit time. You need to care about this when you write your resume for the non-academic employers who do not understand most of the esoteric science or jargon they see on your resume. They will go immediately to the numbers, because employers in all industries understand results expressed objectively in numbers.

Step 2. Get the hardest things out of the way, within the first 2 hours of your waking.

The internet gives you enough distractions to drain away the most productive and mentally alert hours of your day. Make a commitment to get the toughest tasks done within the first 2 hours of waking. These are the phone calls you dread making, applications you hate filling out for the two hundredth time, and follow-up emails you feel sick of writing.

You will be surprised how much of what is hard you can get done when you have the most mental energy at your service. This also gives you items to tally in Step 1.

Step 3. At the end of the week, do an informal performance assessment: what worked, what didn't work?

Maybe there was a phone call that went very well, that made you feel motivated to achieve great things. Maybe there was an email that was short and blunt, that made you feel small and deflated.

Learn to assess what worked and what did not work: these build up your job seeking "skills" in a meaningful way. If you realized that you respond to negative news better after going out for a short walk and clearing your head, you now know one way to manage factors that work against your motivation. If you observed that you have more energy after listening to a motivating piece of music or performance art, you now know one way to prepare yourself before a phone call where your "positive attitude" must be communicated through the phone.

Successful people aren't people who never fail: they fail many times, and they learn what they did that worked and what they did that didn't work, and they use these lessons-learned to increase the odds of their success and reduce the odds of their failures.

Step 4. Touch base with a "source of support" once a week.

Job seeking is a very lonely and isolating phase of life. You feel like everyone else is employed and on track with their careers, while you're left out and spinning your wheels. You may also come across other job seekers who may be frustrated and a source of negativity.

Find a source of support where you can expect to be understood, to receive compassion and understanding when you feel frustrated, to bounce off ideas you may have had over the past week, to ask questions about what was working and what was not working in your approach to job seeking. This source of support may be a friend, a mentor, or even an online forum that has a supportive and positive environment.

When you are isolated, sometimes you may not realize some unproductive thoughts take up more of your mental space than these should, and you may let these weaken you when you are already vulnerable.

Getting in touch with a source of support helps you remember your strengths, go over some approaches that build on the positive contributions you have made in the past, and look at ways to tackle the problem that you may not have thought about. Sometimes, it's nice to have someone listen to you and not judge you.

Step 5. Reward yourself based on effort: not result.

If you're like me, and you are the kind of person who tends to only reward yourself "if and only if" a high-stakes outcome occurs in your favor (for example, "I'll do this nice thing for myself if I get this job" or "I'll buy this when I get an interview"), this is the time to change how you reward yourself.

Reward the effort. Not the result.

This is especially true of job seeking: reward your effort, not the result.

You can reward your result, of course, but when you reward your effort, you learn to rewire what drives your motivation. You can learn to build your motivation on effort versus the result of your effort. This helps reinforce your motivation against elements you can control (effort) instead of elements you cannot control (results based on other people's decisions and market forces).

What You Can Do

Learn to take emotional risks in safe environments. There are different risk-taking muscles you can practice. Public speaking, going up to strangers and initiating conversation, even taking a different route to work. Your objective is to confront the feelings of fear and in particular, fear of looking stupid in front of people.

Here are examples of emotional risks I'd taken:

- Taking public speaking classes. I did this by joining a local club with Toastmasters International, which is very cost-effective, and competing in speech contests

- Taking improvisational ("improv") classes and performing in an improv "showcase" that is open to the public

- Presenting at a conference where I know I am not an expert and where many people in the audience are experts

You don't have to do these because these items were what made *me* uncomfortable – not necessarily what will make *you* uncomfortable. Emotional risks are personal. You can create your own risk-list.

Learn to get through the feelings of failure. The objective is to take emotional risks to have opportunities that make you feel like this:

"I feel mortified right now. Will they stop looking at me already? I know they are all looking at me. I want to burrow a hole in the ground and hide. I can't face these people again, I can't. I bet they are going to call me out as a fraud and haul me off the stage."

Failure teaches resilience. Failure forces us to confront our decision-making process (or lack thereof) and degree of preparation (or lack thereof). Failure reveals our blind spots. Failure shows us what we are most afraid of about ourselves.

What we are most afraid of is usually not the feeling of failing itself, but the accompanying feelings of embarrassment, disappointment, shame, or self-consciousness. People who are successful are rarely those who have never failed – they simply learn to get through those feelings that come with failure. Then they make necessary adjustments to their strategies and tactics. They continue to act and move forward.

For each success, I have experienced failures, sometimes very painful failures, which I had to live through. My most poignant example was my professional failure as a corporate employee.

I had seen what I believed were questionable business practices at a company I'd worked. I wanted to do something about it: to change the norms so that I – and others like me – would not have to go to work wondering, "Is what I'm doing ethical, is this even legal?"

I failed at my goal of changing the norms at the company. In retrospect, if I had been more politically savvy at the work place, had I more social intelligence or emotional intelligence at the time, perhaps I could have gained allies that have more authority and power than I did (translation: in upper-level management) to make those changes.

But I was young, brash, and ambitious. I was rigid in my thinking of how things should change. This failure put me on an entrepreneurial path as a means to accomplish what I was unable to accomplish when I worked as an employee. If I had never failed, then I would not have gained access to new avenues of work or the entrepreneurial experience that has taken me on an incredible professional journey.

Learn to identify how your resilience has improved. When it comes to job seeking and prospecting for a new career, I've found that persistence is key. You need to get mentally tough. You have to deal with constant frustration and rejection, and keep persisting.

This is easier said than done because to build those mental muscles of resilience, you need to tear the very muscles you are looking to build. This means you learn to become more resilient by going through painful experiences of frustration, rejection, and failure.

I used to think that having a tough skin meant never having my feelings hurt or never caring what people think of me or what I do. But I have learned that this is not true, at least for me. A metric of my mental toughness rests on how quickly I am able to bounce back.

Years ago I might have remained upset for weeks about an insult, a perceived injustice, or a personal attack. Now, I've learned to take other people's opinions less personally and give others the benefit of doubt ("Maybe they didn't mean to be rude; maybe they were even trying to help me.") If there was intended negativity, I'd feel upset for a day or two, then I practice moving on.

This doesn't mean that I have complete disregard for what people are saying about me or thinking of me. If you read the first chapter on what I wished I'd learned in graduate school and the section on Approval, you'll see why I don't believe in *what you think of me is none of my business*. But I can move on with my life much faster than I was able to before, when faced with challenges or negativity, without letting other people's behaviors toward me affect my effectiveness and productivity. This is more useful for me as a metric than not caring at all about what other people think.

The concepts I've shared with you in this chapter go beyond PhD career transitions. You will come to find that in business and in life, success comes primarily from preparation and perseverance, but first you need a critical win. Your first critical win is your own mental game of success.

∞

4. GROW YOUR SOCIAL NETWORK

Employers post jobs where they think their ideal candidates will be looking. The problem is that some of the posts that may be suitable alternative PhD careers are never advertised.

Why? You've just read the answer to this question: it is the first sentence.

"...Where they think their <u>ideal candidates</u> will be looking."

Most career sites or job posting channels generally appeal to the masses. When was the last time you opened up the newspaper, flipped to the help wanted section, and saw a job posting from a major corporation that was looking for upper management or regional director level position? On occasion you will see these types of job postings, but not often. The reason is simple.

Even though the job posting on these sites can be thorough, explaining the requirements, the minimal degree needed, and the desired level of experience, the posting will generate hundreds and possibly even thousands of applications from people all over the region – or these days from around the world – who don't meet the minimum basic requirements.

Try spending the majority of your day digging through email after email and letter after letter, looking for the few candidates who are qualified enough for the position for you to contact them via telephone. Don't forget, you still have your job to run as employer or manager, managing your company and managing your people.

Companies have full-time human resource staff whose only job is to dig through piles of applications and read through as many resumes and cover letters as possible, looking for the rare needles in multiplying haystacks.

The larger the company, the less likely it is that they will post coveted career openings on public forums or public sites.

Smaller companies may not be able to afford the staff necessary to dig through bales of applications either and may also shy away from general public postings.

This is why even with the ease of online social networking, the recruiting industry remains a steady source of assistance for companies looking to hire the right people for their positions. This is because recruiters are hired for their networks of job seekers as well as access to referral sources who are usually corporate employees.

There's a real estate adage about the three most important attributes for a property: "Location, location, location." The version of this adage for job seeking success is: "Relationships, relationships, relationships."

In the past, job seekers looked for jobs in the classifieds section of newspapers and asked for referrals from members of their network. Today, job seekers have more options. They can go online to job boards, online classifieds or lists, and social networking sites to ask for referrals from members of their network.

For today's PhDs, the ease of internet access has been as much of a curse as it has been a blessing. **You have a world of job postings at your fingertips. So does your competition.** Every job seeker on the market today with internet access can put themselves in front of the computer monitor, 8 hours a day, 7 days a week, in search of a job opportunity.

PhDs who seek alternative careers face an additional hurdle. There are jobs that you may be suited for, but because employers are not thinking about you as a job candidate, they are not writing the job description with *you* in mind. Instead, employers look for the reliable and familiar profile of job seekers that *they* have in mind.

This reliable and familiar profile will not look like *you*, at least, in the job description that they had written. But just because an employer has not in the past hired a person with a PhD to fill a position does not mean that he will not when he meets you. Why can't *you* be the first PhD hired to the team? I have been "The First PhD Who _____" many times in my career life. You can, too.

As the noise in web-based job seeking increases, matching employers with prospective employees becomes harder.

This means:

- Employers have more difficulty targeting their postings to the right audience of job seekers.

- Employers have more difficulty finding the right candidate for their jobs.

- Job seekers have more difficulty getting their online applications noticed, or preventing their applications from the [Delete] key.

- Job seekers have more difficulty differentiating themselves from the ever-increasing competition.

- Members of a social network receive more requests for referrals from job seekers than ever before.

- Members of a social network who are particularly "well-connected" or are "critical connectors" (critical connects are people who are highly influential and have strategic and high-quality connections) are inundated with requests for connections from job seekers.

Practical Application: Learn to scout from the other side of the job seeking equation. Imagine you are a hiring manager or a recruiter. How are you finding candidates to screen and interview? What websites or social networks do you visit and spend time on?

These places may not be the same places that job seekers hang out. Employers tend to congregate in places where they can share business common problems with their peers to solve. Recruiters may be at these same locations in addition to regular "networking" groups online.

Once you generate a list of ideas of "places where recruiters and employers hang out", go there and observe.

You will have to do significant homework/research and be creative in how you network and become known to prospective employers. The harder your homework is, the more likely your competition is not thinking about doing this or does not do this, and the less competition you will have for the job.

By focusing your efforts on attracting employers, you can change the dynamics of your job search experience. By establishing a unique presence – what the business world may call value proposition or more recently, personal brand – you become a person who attracts employers, rather than a person who seeks out employment opportunities.

Job Seeker versus Attractive Employee

Take a moment and think about this. The desired end result for a person who is job-seeking and a person who is employer-attracting is the same: a job offer.

Yet there is a difference in the strategy and actions of a person who operates as a job seeker versus a person who operates to attract employers. This difference is perceived by most critical connectors in social networks. For example, a job seeker would be seen by critical connectors as a person who kept asking for favors. On the other hand, a person who was attractive to employers will be seen by critical connectors as a person who brought value to their social network and increased the overall net worth of their relationships.

I am not saying stop your job seeking. I'm suggesting that you *reconfigure* your current strategies when prospecting for employment, especially if you are looking for alternative careers.

Ever notice how employers seem to hire people who work at organizations similar to their own – or at least – people who are already employed? This preference is not solely due to employers aiming for candidates with comparable experience, but also because a person who is already attractive to an employer appears attractive to other employers.

Maybe you have personal experience with this phenomenon: When you had a job and you weren't looking for employment, you were fielding calls from recruiters and people you know showered you with job leads. Then when you didn't have a job and really needed one, the calls stopped and the leads dried up.

The same principle works in sales too, with sales people. A sales person who was in a great financial position, who enjoyed the sales process and who did not need to win every single sale seemed to make selling effortless and closed lots of sales. On the other hand, a sales person who was living paycheck-to-paycheck and who needed to win every single sale seemed to repel customers and had a very difficult time closing even the easiest sale.

What is at work here is the effect of desperation on the likelihood of success. Job seekers can behave with a degree of desperation that can be uncomfortable to people that they need to make the most comfortable: critical connectors and employers. Job seekers can come across as wanting something for themselves (a job) and asking for favors up front (leads to jobs, introductions to employers) and having a single-minded focus (themselves). Without a mutual benefit or reciprocation of value, critical connectors find these relationships one-sided and a poor investment of their time. Employers will hide behind generic email addresses to avoid fielding unsolicited job requests.

On the other hand, people who are employed aren't necessarily desperate for a new job. If employees are looking to leave their current employment, they can scout for opportunities at a more deliberate pace; this pace affects the balance of power between employer and prospective employee and makes the employee attractive for a new employer. As a result, employees who are on the job market appear interested but relaxed. They don't always have an agenda when connecting with members of their social network. They can form connections without requesting favors up front. This makes them more attractive to critical connectors who have employment leads.

You can model attractive employee behaviors *without* being employed.

Take a moment and think about this. That thin line between employer aversion and employer attraction comes from the degree of desperation that affects how a person approaches the job market. That degree of desperation is made up of all of a person's actions – big and small – in the job market.

Legal status, employed or unemployed, is not what makes a person appear desperate or not desperate. Instead, a person's *approach* to gaining employment is what makes a person appear desperate or not desperate. You may not always be in control of your employment status, but you are in control of your approach.

Of course, unemployment or unpredictable employment puts tremendous pressure – very real pressure – on anyone, and this causes a person to become desperate. But you remain in control of your behaviors in response to pressure and stressful situations. Not surprisingly, remaining effective under high pressure situations is an aptitude that employers look for in employees and becomes a requirement at higher levels of executive management.

Job seekers who exhibit a calm yet energetic pace about them will appear more attractive to employers than job seekers who come across as flustered, frustrated, aggressive, needy, or pushy. This is because employers only get a snapshot of you as a person from the brief initial impression you give. Employers will take this snapshot and extrapolate it to how you may behave as an employee in their organization.

It's understandable that employers generally prefer to hire other employers' employees to become their own employees: because most job seekers don't look like employees, they look like desperate sales people. Think about the last time when you went to a store and had an overzealous sales person shadowing you, trying to get you buy something, and otherwise ignoring your lack of interest or discomfort. If you were like most customers, the next time you entered that store again, you may either avoid that sales person or quickly turn away with, "No thank you, I am just looking."

If you dread networking because of all the strangers you have to approach and talk to, imagine how critical connectors feel about these networking events. They know that most of the people who approach them probably want something from them. This is one of the reasons why critical connectors disguise themselves as another person in the crowd, there for networking like everyone else.

How do you shift from desperate job seeker to attractive potential employee? By shifting your approach to how you "work your social network". You focus on giving value.

Give Value

The quickest way to reduce stress and pressure in social and networking situations is to stop focusing on what you want and start focusing on what the other person wants. By shifting your intention for being there at the event from "How can I get as many job leads and first names of hiring managers within a 10-minute interval" to "How many people can I find that I can help in some way, either with what I know or with who I know", networking becomes less stressful and even be fun.

When you focus on yourself, you may become more self-conscious in the environment. When you focus on other people, you actually become more interesting to them, without trying to become a more interesting person!

Once I had attended a dinner event that was part of a professional society meeting. I sat down between a consultant and his business partner. I did not know they were business partners or I would have avoided sitting right in the middle of two potential sales pitches. One of them asked me what I did.

When he heard that I owned a business (therefore, a potential client for his business,) he did not give me a sales pitch. Instead, he asked me questions about the industry I worked in, why I decided to start a business, how business was going, and what I may have found challenging as a business owner. He did not ask me if I was interested in buying what he had to sell. He didn't ask me for business referrals up front so he could get names of people in my network who may be interested in buying what he had to sell.

Instead, he gave me value. He gave me suggestions on ways I could improve my business process. He did not make me feel pressure or obligation to listen to a sales pitch about the services his firm provides. By demonstrating his insight about the business development process, he immediately piqued my interest in how he works with small business owners. Since I felt no pressure, I asked how he worked with other business owners to solve their problems. Then I agreed to attend a business breakfast that his company provided to learn more about the services.

Here are some types of value that you can immediately give:

- Data and information

- Knowledge and insight (especially if you are a subject matter expert; PhDs are subject matter experts in their fields)

- Connections to other people in your network

- Creative ideas and thinking

- Serving as a sounding board and/or listening

The last item, serving as a sounding board and/or listening is a value that you can offer no matter where you are in your career or life. This is a simple and underutilized skill for networking even though it's an effective way of making the other person feel like you are paying attention to what he's interested in or cares about.

Whenever job seekers hesitated at my suggestion to give value because they weren't sure what value they could offer, I would remind them that the most important gift they can give to another person is the giving of listening. Many job seekers underestimate the power of giving value without expecting value in return. Humans are conditioned to reciprocate; this is the principle that marketers use when giving away free samples of their products.

If you want to read more about reciprocity and its effect on influence, I highly recommend Robert Cialdini's book, *Influence*. When you focus on giving value, then you will be listening and learning more than you may be speaking, sharing, or teaching. You will be more likely to come across an opportunity where you may offer value in a way that only you can offer it, which differentiates you from other job seekers. This means that you can focus more on what value you can give, and fully engage in your conversation with the other person rather than wondering in the back of your mind, "How is this going to benefit me in the future?"

Identify Your Unique Contribution

If you aren't already aware, now is the time to identify what is unique about how you do what you do: Your unique contribution to your work, your field and industry, and your unique contribution to the world. This goes beyond what you know because information can be acquired by anyone who is willing and able to acquire it, and does not differentiate you from someone else with access to the same information. *What makes your contribution unique is what you do with what you know, and how you do it.*

Identifying your unique contribution may be an ongoing and gradual process. It took me several years to identify my unique contribution, which includes using lessons learned from my personal experience to shorten others' learning curve so they can succeed faster and more cost-effectively. In other words, I don't want you to have to learn the lessons I've had to learn the hard way if you can use some of the best practices I have identified and put these to work for your own success. I do this by sharing personal stories with you and by asking questions to help you "self-discover" throughout this book.

Your unique contribution is related to, but different, from talent or your strengths. You can be tremendously talented and others will never know about your talents unless you've done something with your talent that others can see or benefit from in some way.

The cellist Yo Yo Ma is a prodigious musician, but his unique contribution has been using music as a tool to bring diverse cultures together, which differentiates him from other musicians who may use their musical talents differently. Ma's unique contribution garnered him an appointment in 2006 as United Nations' Messenger of Peace. I have an artist friend who used her art as a healing tool to help women and children who are victims of domestic violence; she founded an organization in 1991 that has since grown to provide art workshops for hundreds of thousands of women and children who otherwise have not been able to express the traumatic experiences they had lived through. My friend used art as a way to express herself because she grew up painfully shy; now her unique contribution is helping women and children in profound ways.

I was recently working with a retired professional football player, discussing the strategies of one of his business ventures. A huge entertainment company wanted him to lead a major project that was part of a new stadium being built. We talked about his personal brand that has led to this potential opportunity. The entertainment company had approached three different people for recommendations on who should lead this project. Each of the three people recommended to the company this same sport celebrity as the right person for the job. I used this opportunity to help him identify his unique contribution by asking this question:

"What question do you think the company asked each of the three references that made them say your name instead of someone else's name?"

He identified his long history of focusing on community activism, being dedicated to player safety and advocating for ethical decision-making in business as factors that differentiated him from other equally qualified candidates that the company may have otherwise approached for the job. This question helped him clarify not only why he may be qualified for the job, but more importantly, what differentiated him from others who may be equally qualified for the same position.

What about you? Imagine a prospective employer went to three different people in your social network, and asked each of them a question about the right person for a particular job. What would the question be, such that the only natural recommendation that each of these three people can give would be *Your Name*?

Remember the Power of "One"

Have you ever felt alone even when you are in a room full of people? Consider the logistics of forming a new social connection. When you find yourself among a large group of people at a networking event, you have to effectively isolate the signal from a lot of noise. Then you have to identify a starting point to make a new connection without feeling overwhelmed by the sheer number of people around you.

Once you've identified someone you'd like to approach, you have to walk toward him. As you make your approach, you are on heightened alert for clues of his level of reception toward you. Is he still smiling? Is he still looking at you? Or has he reached into his pocket and is pretending to check his phone messages? Even if he appeared friendly and receptive at your approach, your work has only just begun: Now you have to engage him in a conversation!

When you consider the sheer number of steps you must take before ever engaging someone at a networking event, and many opportunities for rejection even before you begin to talk to someone, it's no wonder that many people dread the very idea of networking.

I for one am not a master networker — but I know many master networkers! One master networker has even built an entire business from the sheer value of his network: he earns referral fees by matching a buyer within his network with a service provider or seller within his network. These people create revenue streams from their network.

When I asked master networkers what networking is about, first they tell me about the common misconceptions of networking. They said that networking is not about how many business cards or how many email addresses you can collect. Networking is not about how many times you can give your "elevator pitch" about who you are and why you are there.

Instead, networking is paying attention to one person at a time, one conversation at a time. Master networkers can make the other person feel like that person is the most important person in the room. Master networkers are fully engaged in the conversation and show intense interest in what the other person is sharing. They rarely pitch their services but will readily share value in an initial conversation.

If networking is a forum for you to give value first, then you need to find out what the other person is interested in and why he is there. If you don't know how the other person is looking to enrich his social network, you would not be able to have the key information you need to offer your unique contribution.

You are looking to build your social network, one relationship at a time. Leverage the power of one. Focus on one person at a time, one conversation at a time. When you focus on "one" you can shift the way you network and find that networking can be enjoyable and effective.

Practical Application: Take a blank sheet of paper or a notebook and list 8-10 ways you "give value" in a work place. You can use your current and/or previous work place as a starting point for this exercise.

How do you make the work place more effective and productive?

How do you make your boss's job easier?

The way we give value is unique and may not be readily appreciated: for example, if you have a reputation as "the glue that holds the team together", this is a very important way you give value to the workplace.

Think about this statement:

"{*Your name*} is the person I recommend to solve these problems and make this happen at your company."

Brainstorm on what "these problems" are.

Brainstorm on what you are best at "making happen" at an organization, regardless of industry.

Contact a trusted peer or a mentor and go over your list. Ask for feedback. Sometimes other people can see more ways you give value than what you give yourself credit for.

Grow Your Luck

In 2006, I worked with a life coach who insisted that I schedule time each week for a hobby. I had signed up for professional development classes to improve my business skills, which I enjoyed, but the coach said that these weren't done for fun. Since I have a tendency to want to control everything, the coach suggested that I take comedy improvisational classes. I didn't know what I was getting into when I signed up for beginner improv classes with the local community adult school.

The first night in class, I was terrified. My palms were sweaty, my knees shook, and I wondered if it was too late to drop the class. Like most

49

beginners, I was very concerned about how I could plan what I'd do in a scene. But improv gives no time for planning; I wouldn't know what character I would play until I was on stage receiving instructions from the director and members of the audience.

After a few classes, I began to understand why the director kept drilling us on listening skills and cultivating the attitude of, "Yes, and...!" The key to performing well at an improv game is to *not* have a game plan. Every second I used for premeditation was a precious second I'd lost for listening to cues and clues from my acting partner, the director, the audience, the environment, and from *myself*.

How does this relate to growing your luck? Luck acts the same way as an improv game. If you get the outcome you desired by working a plan, then you wouldn't say that you were lucky. People who were transfixed on a spot on the job seeking stage often missed clues that were vital to their odds of getting lucky.

The first key in growing your luck is listening. Listen fully. Listen without judgment. Listen without planning what you will say next or how you will say it. You can always ask for a minute to compose your thoughts, the other person may even appreciate the care you are taking before speaking your mind.

Richard Wiseman, a psychologist professor at the University of Hertfordshire who studies luck, said that the harder people looked for a certain result, the less they saw of ready opportunities for luck. In "The Luck Factor", an article Wiseman published in the May/June 2003 issue of Skeptical Inquirer, Wiseman said that unlucky job seekers "...look through newspapers determined to find certain types of job advertisements, and as a result miss other types of jobs."

Wiseman used a simple experiment to test how readily people noticed chance opportunities. He gave self-proclaimed lucky and unlucky people a newspaper. He asked each group to look through the newspaper and find out the number of photographs inside. Lucky people took a few seconds to complete the experiment while unlucky people took a few minutes to complete the same experiment.

What accounted for this difference in response time? Lucky people found on the second page of the newspaper a message that stated, "Stop counting, there are 43 photographs in this newspaper!" Unlucky people, on the other hand, missed seeing this message because they were busy counting photographs in the same newspaper.

The second key of a good improv actor is the same as the second key in growing luck: respond to what you were given by saying, "Yes, and..."

For example, if I were given the role of a car mechanic in an improv scene but I didn't even know how to change the tires on a car.

Instead of saying, "I can't be a mechanic, I don't know my way around a spare tire," I could accept the role that I was given and build from there. I could say, "Yes, I am a car mechanic, and... I had just flunked out of car mechanic school but I want to work on cars even if I can't tell a lug from a nut!" This scene is rich with possibilities of a mechanically challenged car mechanic set on realizing his passion!

Again, this is a matter of orienting focus and energy. If I spent my energy on denying what I was given, I'd tie up energy from creating on what I was given. By saying, "Yes, and..." I challenged myself to build on what showed up instead of lamenting what bad luck I had been having. This is in essence the same principle that Wiseman described as, "...adopting a resilient attitude that turns bad luck into good luck."

In fact, it was by luck that I found out about Wiseman's work while writing this section of this chapter. I wasn't looking for scientific studies on luck; I wanted to relate my own experiences with luck and ways that I grew my own luck, particularly within the context of growing a valuable social network. But I had signed up with a blogging website to write about personal finance – an activity that I was interested in more as a hobby ("fun!") than as a business activity.

On the day that I logged into my account, one of the personal finance blogs that I followed happened to share a link about lucky people. The link led to another website that showed the article on luck that Wiseman had written. If I hadn't started blogging about personal finance, I wouldn't have signed up for a new blog account, and I would not have checked in that day and glanced through the blog dashboard. I would never have seen the link to Wiseman's article that has added useful information on how to grow luck. I got lucky!

"Net Worth" of Your Social Network

A key step in building a social network is to define what are the variables of "worth" you want to track from the network that you build.

When I look at my social network, for example, I am less interested in the number of people I have in my network than the quality of the relationships and the potential for mutually beneficial results.

For example, my variables for "worth" in a social network are:

- Type of experience a person has

- Thought leadership or level of expertise in an industry

- Capacity for critical thinking

- Character and authenticity

- X-Factor

I am not necessarily looking for the same type of experience that I have. I look for work and life experiences that I find interesting because one of my objectives for growing my social network is to broaden my horizons and learn from diverse experiences and industries.

I look for level of mastery or thought leadership in one's chosen industry or life path: this creates engaging and insightful conversations. I enjoy critically thinking of a problem; therefore I appreciate people with a capacity for critical thinking. These variables allow me to create a network of industry insight as well as insights to life and decision-making, which fosters a real competitive advantage as I grow as a professional.

Since I'm invested in long-term social relationships, I value character and authenticity. A person who has character will be authentic in his portrayal of himself, what he believes in and what values he stands for. This is a person that I can do business on a hand-shake and mutual trust.

The "X-factor" is harder to define; it's not a trait or a skill or a type of personality. Something about this person has caught my attention – maybe it was the question that he had asked or the language he used when he answered a question.

What has been interesting is that many of the people in my social network have similar values as mine. One of my contacts, a critical connector that I first met in 2005, invited me into a new business venture that he has created; I am one of the first 7 people he has invited to participate in the new business idea. This core nucleus of participants included thought leaders in their respective areas of leadership development, corporate training, social media consulting, and marketing.

The critical connector told me that he selected each participant based on the level of trust, integrity, and confidence that allowed us to do business "on a handshake." This does not mean that we do not have legal contracts in place; it speaks to the desired participation profile.

Another contact is a person that I had added to my network in November 2009 but we reconnected more than a year later. He continued monitoring my professional activities and the information I shared online. I wrote something that caught his attention, and he reached out to have a telephone conversation to discuss what he had read. Our conversation ultimately led to a business introduction with a critical connector within his network, which led to a business project with high potential for launching me into a new industry and even new fields of work.

This approach to social networking has worked well for me. Even though it may take a longer time for the value of my social network to "vest", the degree of value can be very high: these would include major business relationships, large scale projects, or even joint ventures that propel me into a new career path.

Let's Talk About Trust

Being able to define and identify for yourself how you can trust a person in a professional or business capacity is crucial to your survival at the workplace. Maybe you can think of examples in your own work life where you thought you could trust a person, and you were mistaken, and how this mistake created complex problems that drained much of the creative energy and time you would otherwise devote to work. Just as you don't want to work in a place where you can't or don't trust anyone (you don't want to go through life this way, either), you need to formulate a list of "signs I can trust this person."

Here are 5 guideposts or signs that I use for gauging trustworthiness:

One. This person is not afraid to tell me the truth when it is in my best interest, even if he may lose my business or my friendship for fear of my becoming upset enough to shoot the messenger. I will share a personal story at the end of this section, about this point.

Two. This person is willing to give me multiple alternatives or solutions to my question or problem, which includes options of "not listening to me (the person), or giving me business, or giving me some form of business advantage."

Three. This person believes and behaves on, "Inaction or silence is in itself, an action and a decision that affects someone's business or someone's life." In both the personal and business world, many people have been harmed, ruined, delayed, or mislead when a "nice" person chooses to say nothing or do nothing, either because they think "this isn't my problem, this isn't my business" or "I'm not going to be the messenger who gets shot". Acquaintances who do this, I'll let slide. But anyone who has ever crossed into my mental model as "a friend" does not get away with this and remain a friend of mine (this is also the reason why I have very few friends, and I accept this).

Four. This person acts consistently with his self-proclaimed priorities. I'm fine with people making careless mistakes. We're human beings; I've made plenty of careless mistakes. But when I see a person's actions in real life, often contradicting what the person says as his or her modus operandi that is an inconsistency.

This makes me wonder if:

- this person does not have a capacity to behave as he claims,

- this person is showing an act, which differs from the person's actions,

- this person is getting something from the act, which for many is "gaining attention and approval"

Five. A trusted person does NOT set off my gut checks ("red flags") and does not go out of his or her way to make my gut "wrong". They can present different alternatives and let me think through my decision.

Now, my "shoot the messenger" story as promised from the previous page. I had a couple of business colleagues, who had known each other for many years before I came into the picture. We each come with our expertise, and one of us (not me) is "the star"; the star is a celebrity in his industry. I, and the other colleague, bring "the star" our differential strengths, to help his cause.

Over time I became troubled with the other colleague. And more troubled. I had grave concerns about what I suspected was happening with this other colleague, which was the colleague leveraging the star's name for his own business gain without informing the star of all the different ways he was doing this. He even made a YouTube video for another organization, dropping the star's name, without informing the star about the video.

I had to think very carefully about the ramifications of what I was about to do. But there was never a question in my mind of whether I should say something to the star who has explicitly told me that he trusted me. I said a variation of this to him: "Because I know you trust me, I believe it is my duty to tell you, that this is what I am seeing. I may be wrong and I am happy to be proven wrong. If don't say anything about what I see as extremely troubling to me, then I feel I have violated your trust. But a person who keeps trying to persuade you that your gut instinct is wrong is not your friend."

I took no pleasure in being right: "Jane, you were right, I feel so disappointed in this person." But I was relieved that this happened soon enough than too late, and that I said something.

What You Can Do

Step 1. Choose a social network that you want to practice for this exercise.

In time you can expand this technique to multiple social networks, but to start, focus on one social network. I have used LinkedIn with good results, for example.

If you are already involved in a social network, build on what you already have. You can always expand to additional social networks, but keep in mind that creating visibility and momentum within even one social network can be a major time investment.

Step 2. Choose one channel within the social network that you want to focus on.

For example, you can target one LinkedIn "group" and/or one topical area of LinkedIn Answers.

I tend to favor LinkedIn Groups because the topics may be contained within the group and seen by the members of the group. LinkedIn Answers are open to all of LinkedIn and your answers may not be seen the same groups of people unless they start to "follow" you.

Step 3. Identify ways of giving value and showing your unique contribution.

This can mean answering questions and engaging in a discussion that moves the conversation forward or enriches the discussion with your own insight.

This can also mean that you bring a quality to the conversation that is unique to you, for example, if you ask questions that encourage deeper examination of issues that others have not considered before, this becomes your unique contribution.

Step 4. Track your activities and results.

You don't need to count the number of answers you give or how many connections you make per week. You can track activities that are meaningful to you and the results that tell you that you are on the right track. I don't track the number of connections in my network as a metric. I do track the level of activity I generate as a result of answering a question, such as the number of comments specific to my response, or direct conversations from people interested in my response. The most objective metric that I track is in dollars – the value of a project that has resulted from an activity or the potential of a new business that was a direct result of a conversation.

For job seekers, comparable metrics would be the number of queries you may receive from critical connectors or prospective employers. This is different from the number of queries you put forth to prospective employers; remember we are looking to shift from job seeking to employer attracting.

Step 5. Take time and really think about what is important for you when you grow your social network:

Answer these questions for your social network:

- What sort of value are you looking to give to and gain from your social network?

- What value can you focus on giving up front?

- What is your unique contribution?

- When do you need to see a return on your investment?

- What are your short term and long term objectives for your social network?

- What social networks will you consistently give value to and build your visibility?

∞

5. PUT YOURSELF IN EMPLOYERS' SHOES

Many job seekers look at their job search through a one-way mirror. They think they know that they have what it takes to succeed if only they were giving the chance. What they often miss is the perspective of the people on the other side of the mirror: Employers who conduct numerous interviews, looking for the most suitable candidate for the position. Job seekers often miss competitors vying for the same job and how they differentiated themselves in their bid for the same offer.

I want you to take a short journey with me. Imagine that you were walking into a job interview.

Don't sit down yet, at least, not where you would usually sit. Move around the desk and settle down behind the large, brilliantly finished oak desk, where the hiring manager sat. Breathe in that massive symbol of power and feel the wood beneath your fingers. Performance awards and letters of recognition – yours as the hiring manager – were framed and hanging on the wall behind you; these proved that you had earned your place at the desk.

Let's give you, the hiring manager, a little background. You graduated from college, maybe top in your class. When you landed your job, you quickly realized that you had a lot to learn about the real world of business. You worked diligently and frequently volunteered to work weekends in a cubicle. You "paid your dues," and did all of the things that people do when they wanted to move up the rungs of the corporate ladder. Over the years, you worked your way conscientiously up the corporate ladder.

The company's upper management recognized your determination and dedication. They saw the results you had delivered consistently and noticed that you had become a positive influence to your peers at the organization. Several promotions later, you had become a director of a major department. Now you had the large desk in an executive office. You had a budget. You had headcount! This meant you had open positions to fill. You aimed to support the company's expansion and an enterprise-wide effort to improve short-term performance and bolster long-term competitiveness in a saturated market. Hiring the right talent would be a start to differentiating your company from its competitors.

You saw the stack of resumes on your desk and you knew the work ahead of you: You had been through this a hundred times in your prior junior management positions and assisting your director in hiring. Today you would conduct interviews all day while catching up on administrative tasks during your short breaks. You have five candidates coming in. Two of these candidates worked for your competition and one of them had been with the same company for over five years. The other had a master's degree and a year's worth of experience in the field.

One applicant has a bachelor's degree and experience in a different field; you were looking to hire applicants with advanced degrees but his application caught your eye. This applicant had been volunteering in a non-profit organization that your company had a history of supporting through company-matched donations. The applicant was also in the process of earning a master's degree; it appeared that he was juggling full time work, volunteering, and education.

The final two applicants had PhD degrees. One applicant was a few years out as a PhD and was a postdoctoral fellow. The other had just graduated with a PhD. Many of your employees had master's degrees and one of them is in the process of earning a PhD degree, but you have not yet hired a PhD on board with your team. You were open to the idea of adding a PhD-trained employee to your team, but you did not know what to expect.

The first applicant – your first interview of the morning – was the postdoctoral fellow.

The postdoctoral fellow walked into your office with an air of confidence. He extended his hand and you shook it; you liked his firm handshake. You offered him a seat across your desk. He thanked you and you couldn't help but like him immediately.

You began your interview with a predictable question, "Tell me why you are interested in this position." The applicant explained his interest in industry and your organization's business; he was able to cite specific business activities that your company had been involved in (especially when it had invested in a media campaign to grow public awareness). So far, so good; you continued with the next question.

"What makes you think you are qualified for this job?" You asked.

Some of your peers had told you that the way you asked this question was too blunt and could scare off job applicants, but you didn't believe in sugarcoating questions. You also used this question to gauge how candidates responded to your directness. You wanted to hire people who were compatible with your management style.

The applicant said, "I read the job description and I know I can do the tasks that the job requires, I'm used to managing a large amount of data and analyzing this information."

The applicant began to describe a recent research project and what he had done; you weren't familiar with his topical expertise and weren't sure how these related to the job you were interviewing him for. But you paid attention and tried to make sense of what his accomplishments were and how these may relate to this open position. The applicant continued talking and you realized that he was going down his resume, explaining the details of each research project and the publications that resulted.

"Why do you think you are a good fit for this job?" You asked another version of the same question; you weren't sure that you understood the answer the first time around, if the applicant had indeed answered your question. You didn't understand a lot of the jargon he had used because you were not familiar with his field of expertise.

The applicant said that he liked working with people and that he was a people-person. The applicant says that he is certain he can do the work required of the position. Then he reviewed the job description and assured you that he was confident that he could perform the tasks outlined in the job description.

You felt a little disappointed. You decided to pull out the final litmus test. This was a statement and not a question, but the applicant's response to this statement would extend – or end – the interview.

"I need people who can hit the ground running, a person who can pick up the ball and run with it. I don't have a lot of resources to train someone without experience." With this statement, you leaned back and watched the applicant's reaction.

The applicant leaned back too, which you didn't view as a good sign; still, you kept your facial expression neutral. The applicant looked a bit deflated, his confident smile fading a little. When he spoke he sounded a little frustrated, as if he had said these words many times before:

"I know I don't have direct experience in this job, but this is why I'm applying to this job. I know I have what it takes to do this job and be successful if you'll give me a chance to prove myself," he said, his voice hinting impatience.

You thanked the applicant and sent him on his way. You marked that applicant's application as rejected – applicant is overqualified but under-experienced for the position.

You were sure that the applicant was extremely intelligent and probably very capable of doing the work you were hiring for, but your company wasn't in the business of investing in unproven talent. At least, not right now, when competition is fierce and you needed people who could deliver results right away. You simply couldn't take this risk right now.

Did you find this story of the role reversal familiar, only you were the PhD job seeker who had heard many times the familiar "overqualified, underexperienced" objection?

A more likely scenario would be the situation taking place over the telephone, as opposed to occurring in person, with a recruiter or a staffing consultant with the company, as opposed to the hiring manager. I used an in-person scenario to make the example more vivid.

In recent years there has been increased hiring of PhD applicants in certain job markets, such as financial markets embracing PhDs in mathematics. However, employers in alternative job markets have indeed shied away from hiring PhD applicants partly because they did not always understand the value of a PhD.

Not all employers would be willing to take a risk and hire PhD applicants if they could not readily understand how well PhD applicants could fit in as members of their teams.

This means the burden of proof is with you, the job applicant with the PhD degree. You are responsible for making sure that everything you communicate during a job interview is clear and understood by the employer, from the examples you used to demonstrate your transferable experience to the jargon that you used.

The first step is to put yourself in the interviewers' position and see yourself, your accomplishments, and your weaknesses through their eyes. If you suspect that the employer believes that hiring PhD applicants is a risky proposition, how can you turn your application into a risk-worth-taking from the employer's point of view?

When an employer says that you're overqualified, the employer isn't worrying about all the knowledge you bring to the organization given your advanced education. Wouldn't we naturally want to hire the best, the smartest, and the most-educated person for any position?

Practical Application: Carry through the imaginary scenario at the start of this chapter, with you as the hiring manager, interviewing a PhD job seeker.

What specific examples would you want to hear from this PhD job seeker, to make you more comfortable making a hiring decision?

How will you defend your hiring decision from skeptical internal stakeholders, who may question whether you are making a sound investment in a hire?

How will you defend your hiring decision from members of your current team who may feel threatened or insecure about having a PhD degree holder as a new team member?

Now, what will you do as the PhD job seeker to build the assets and skills you need to make this happen in your favor?

What "Overqualified" Really Means

We all want the best value and the best deals whether we are buying or hiring. Why would an employer walk away from a potentially great deal in hiring a PhD? **Because the employer believes that hiring a PhD for this particular position would not be a good return on investment (ROI).** The employer thinks that the risks of hiring a PhD will outweigh whatever rewards the employer may gain from having a PhD aboard the team, whether or not these risks are justified.

Since employers sink heavy costs in time and money to hire and train an employee, employers also consider retention when making hiring decisions. In the case of an applicant who appears overqualified, an employer may believe that the applicant is using this position as a stepping stone, or a training position, to gain experience and to improve the applicant's marketability for another position for which the applicant may be appropriately qualified.

Employers get a bad deal if they hire and train a PhD applicant only to have that person gain experience and then leave for "better opportunities".

Employers also consider the consequences of hiring a PhD applicant to a team whose members may not have advanced degrees. There may be costs involved in managing conflicts that may arise from team members. Anytime a new hire comes aboard a team, there is temporary instability as members of the team acclimate to working with a new person and a new personality. When the new hire is significantly different in qualification, this instability may be amplified. Some members of the team who may already feel insecure about their position at the team may feel threatened. They may wonder if this would be the first of a pattern of hiring trends, whether team members without advanced degrees may be replaced with applicants with advanced degrees.

Outside the academic world, and in a corporate setting, one's approach to communication is often judged as a sign of one's interpersonal skills and emotional intelligence. What one intends as an unbiased challenge in a discussion may be perceived by another as a personal attack based on the way that the challenge is communicated. Instability may also be worsened if the newly hired PhD creates conflict or friction with other members of the team by appearing arrogant, when the PhD is used to the critical style of academic debates.

Employers are not always be willing to step out of their comfort zones and seriously consider PhD applicants without a clear understanding of the risks and rewards of introducing a different background to their teams. Employers will not always tell you the real reason for their concern: you will have to uncover the true objections yourself.

To uncover true objections, you have to know how to handle objections. Knowing how to handle objections is one of the most important skills you can gain, but you will probably not learn this in school or even on the job unless you go into a sales job where facing objections and rejections are part of your daily business.

When we hear that we're overqualified for the job, our immediate reaction is to show why this is wrong. Why wouldn't employers hire the most qualified for this job or even more qualified than the job needs? The fastest way to get people to dig in their heels and hold onto their beliefs is to make them wrong. When some people feel they are made wrong, they withdraw and get defensive. In an interview situation when they are the people making hiring decisions, your "win" usually makes you lose.

Uncovering the True Objection
Imagine that a friend called you to go out to lunch. For the past few weeks you'd been equally splitting the lunch bill even though the friend consistently ordered the most expensive items on the menu. You told your friend that you were going to be very busy the next few weeks and have to work through lunch.

Working through lunch was not the reason why you hesitated in saying yes to the lunch invitation. Wanting a fairer split of the bill was your true objection. You weren't sure how to tell your friend what was really bothering you, so you gave a reason that didn't make you too uncomfortable. Employers can be the same way.

Employers don't want to tell you the truth because the truth may be a difficult conversation, and one they may not feel comfortable in discussing with job applicants. If an employer had a negative experience with an employee and that employee has a PhD degree, the employer may not want to discuss that past experience because of confidentiality issues. Even if there were no confidentiality issues to keep employers from telling applicants their true concerns, they may hold back because they knew that the applicant may try to change their minds.

The first step in uncovering the true objection is to not make employers' opinions wrong: the employers' opinions make perfect sense to them, even if you perceive these opinions as based on faulty logic. Since you would probably not know the entirety of the situation upon which they had formed their opinion, you could not effectively change their minds.

Instead, try this radical but easy approach: agree with them!

Nod your head and agree that, from the employer's perspective, you may indeed be overqualified for the position. If you don't make employers wrong about their point of view, then they will not raise their defenses. This gives you a chance to uncover what employers are truly worried about when considering a PhD applicant for the position.

The second step is for you to choose among available options of re-engagement: after hearing the superficial objection, you have options: You can thank the employer and part ways, you can stay and try to find out what the true objections are, or you can move the conversation forward in any meaningful way.

If the employer is obviously not interested in spending more time with you, save yourself the frustration by thanking him and moving on. If this is an event at a career fair where you have approached an employer, then you may encounter a genuine lack of interest from the employer in shifting his current hiring practices. This is part of your job seeking process. You should expect a certain percentage of "No's" when you approach people. Instead of feeling bad about this "no", remember what I talked about in the previous chapters about measuring the "right" things such as effort and action, not the other person's response. If you haven't encountered your fair share of "no's" then you are probably not approaching enough people.

On the other hand, if an employer has approached you, there is something about your background and experience that the employer found interesting. This is usually a sign that you can try to uncover the true objections or move the conversation forward in a meaningful way. In this situation, I wouldn't take "No" at face value and move on. I would stay and uncover the true reasons for the employers' hesitation to move forward with my job candidacy.

The third step is to follow through with your option, and if you choose to stay engaged, to find out the true objection. If you become skilled at continuing the conversation without raising the other person's defenses, you may uncover the true objections in the process.

One method of keeping an employer engaged is by building on the original objection. This means you symbolically move away from your side of the table as the job seeker and move to the employer's side of the table. This is why we went through the role-play earlier in this chapter, so you become more familiar with the employer's perspective.

Talk to the employer as if you were also the employer. You would be objectively assessing the situation and looking for the reasons to agree with him about the risks with hiring a PhD applicant.

You may say, "I understand how hiring a PhD applicant can be risky. There are many challenges when introducing a new hire with a PhD degree to the team."

You stop talking and wait.

If you have established rapport with the employer, he may take your lead and elaborate on his past experiences with hiring PhD applicants or concerns he may have of hiring a PhD applicant to the team.

Maybe in the past, he had hired a PhD applicant and it caused conflict with members of the team who may feel threatened by the new hire because no one else had an advanced degree.

Maybe he had once hired a PhD applicant and took great pains to mentor and train the person only to lose the person once he had become "more marketable".

Maybe he wanted to have a PhD professional on board, but he was not sure whether he would have the resources or the means to train and mentor the person; he may even feel a bit overwhelmed by this challenge.

But you won't find out the real reasons unless the employer believes that you see his point of view and is willing to continue the conversation with you. If you are able to re-engage and find out the true objections, you may choose to either take this information to the next interview, where you may prepare your strategy in overcoming the overqualified-underexperienced objection. Or, you may try to turn the tide in the same interview.

Practical Application: Social situations are fertile for opportunities practice perspective-taking and getting to the root cause of a position. When you are confronted with a dissenting opinion, go through the steps and discover the root cause of the disagreement.

Focus on managing your initial reflex when the other person disagrees or objects. We are conditioned to want to get the other person to agree or see from our perspective: this is the conditioning I want you to practice managing.

One of the "hacks" is to train yourself to take that person's perspective and "agree" and then work your way through to the root cause of a person's assumptions or opinions.

What You Can Do

In speaking with employers who had hired PhDs and may have reservations about hiring employees with advanced degrees, I have heard one or more reasons from the list of true objections.

The true objections behind the overqualified objection may include:

- The employer cannot see, or does not understand, your transferable experience.

- The employer does not believe you'll stay in the job very long.

- The employer does not believe you'll fit into its corporate culture.

- The employer believes that it will cost too much to hire and train you for the job.

- The employer may have been "burned before" from taking a similar risk with a PhD hired.

- The employer does not believe you are actually qualified for the job.

If you know this is a 1- or 2-year job for you, you can be honest about your intentions, but share how you can make this a worthwhile risk to employers even if they only have you on the team for a year or two.

Being honest this way does not guarantee that the employer will take the risk; in fact, it confirms what the employer already fears! The truth is, even if you aren't honest, the employer is already thinking it. You become the memorable job candidate by being honest and proactive – and by expressing your sincerity in wanting to find a mutually beneficially outcome where you get the job and the employer gets his investment's worth.

You may never know how you may cross paths with this employer again in the future. Every opportunity you have right now is part of your long term reputation-building. You may impress an employer enough where he may recommend you to a colleague who is ready to hire PhDs on board; again, you never know!

Once you have uncovered the true objection, you can:

- Show how you can immediately contribute to the organization.

- Show how you've successfully managed people-conflicts in the past: Show how you were able to defuse defenses and prejudices from others who may be threatened because you have a PhD and they don't, and create a collaborative environment with these types of peers.

- Show how your career path may grow with the company: Show how your personal/professional values are congruent with the company's values and culture.

- Show how you can ensure business continuity by mentoring or training potential successors to your job.

One objection that I did not list is that some employers may indeed hold a *personal bias* against PhD applicants. Maybe the person dropped out of his graduate program and this was a painful personal setback. Maybe the person wanted to get a PhD but couldn't for some reason. Maybe the person had such a negative experience with a PhD applicant that he generalized this negativity to all PhD holders.

These are personal reasons that are arbitrary and beyond your control. In these situations you need to move on and focus your energy elsewhere, because this may turn into a working relationship where you would have to prove yourself every single step of the way. Ideally, you want to work for a supervisor who is your ally and biggest supporter. Starting a job where you are constantly being scrutinized or watched isn't ideal.

In any career transition you will encounter situations where you cannot take personally a rejection, even if it stings and feels like a personal affront. This takes a lot of practice, but you are looking to remain focused, productive, and effective when it counts the most.

∞

6. NO EXPERIENCE? GET SOME!

In one of my consultancies, I work in the medical science liaison (MSL) field in the biopharmaceutical industry. I was employed as a MSL for a few years before starting a consulting company in 2004. I couldn't find any articles on MSLs on the internet so I wrote articles about medical science liaisons and the role. This was long before the profession became the coveted career it is today, and more than 5 years before CNN Money named the medical science liaison career as one of 2007's "10 jobs: Big demand, good pay."

Life science professionals who learned about this niche healthcare career began asking me questions about the MSL career when they read my articles. After answering the same types of questions over and over again, I created MSL career products to help aspiring MSLs break into this career. The reason why I'm telling you this is because the number one challenge that almost all aspiring MSLs face is **not having MSL experience**.

Most MSL job postings required the applicant to have prior MSL experience. How could anyone ever get MSL experience without first getting the job?

So infamous was this conundrum that I wrote a book called, "All MSLs Started with No Medical Science Liaison Experience." This no-experience trap was especially pernicious for PhDs, because most come from a non-clinical, basic science background. These PhDs are competing with applicants who are clinicians, holding doctorate degrees in pharmacy or medicine, as well as non-doctoral applicants who have many years of pharmaceutical industry experience.

Because the MSL job is typically ranked at the mid-level management position, there are fewer openings per company than the other better-known field-based position: pharmaceutical sales. Most PhD applicants weren't interested in sales anyway, especially now that more and more PhDs learn about – and apply to – the MSL career. Every single new MSL job posting drew hundreds of applicants.

At any given time, a job market in a particular industry can be an employers' market or a job seekers' market. When there are too many job seekers to choose from, the employers can make specific demands for a particular profile of job seekers they want to hire. When there are too many jobs to fill, the job seekers can make specific demands for a particular profile of employers they want to join.

Since the mid 2000's, the MSL career became an employers' market. There weren't many MSL positions open and there were more and more applicants per vacant position. Until recently, PhD applicants were not native to the MSL job market, which makes the entry barrier into the MSL career a great case study for PhDs looking to overcome the under-experienced objection.

Every Employee Started with No "Experience"
Every first employee in the world started with no experience in their jobs. This is true from entry level positions to mid-level management positions to top executive-level positions.

Employers use "We want prior experience" as an excuse when:

- The current job market is an employers' market and there are many applicants with the existing experience that employers demand.

- Employers have limited resources to train applicants new to the field or industry.

- Employers do not wish to invest in training applicants who may have high potential for success but who does not have transferable experience.

Each of the above-listed reasons accounted for what happened with the MSL job market. Employers complained about being inundated with too many job applications for each MSL job opening. At the same time, employers complained about not having enough qualified candidates for their MSL job openings. Some companies used recruiting agencies hoping for better results, and those recruiters ran into the same problems that the employers did.

71

This is the strategy that I used to help aspiring MSL applicants become visible to employers: Demonstrate Insight and Prove Your Transferable Experience.

How well did this strategy work? I wrote the book in July of 2009. I picked a terrible year to test my strategy, because 2009-2010 were the toughest economic times the world had seen due to the 2007-2008 global financial crises. When companies were short on cash, they liquidated their most expensive cost-centers first, and MSL programs looked very expensive. Many MSLs had been laid off in 2009 and some were still unemployed more than a year later. One MSL told me that after almost 10 years as a MSL and weathering several job market turmoil, he was quitting the MSL career altogether.

In a 12-month period between late-2009 to 2010, my MSL career book helped aspiring MSLs get collectively over $1 Million Dollars-worth of salaries from *new employment* as medical science liaisons. These were people who looked like they stood no chance if they were competing for MSL jobs on the basis of having prior MSL experience.

"Demonstrating insight and proving your transferable experience" is a strategy that works, either for breaking into the MSL career or for competing for alternative PhD careers. I know, because I have done this many times, not only to break into the pharmaceutical sales career or the medical science liaison career, but also to start my consulting business and getting clients to keep my business viable and successful.

If you can create the strategy and action plans for yourself *you don't need to buy my books – or any "MSL/career books" to create results for yourself*

Information versus Insight

There are versions of an anecdote that I'm about to tell you, but the lesson is the same. A CEO of a major corporation was wondering whether he should acquire another corporation as part of a competitive strategy. The CEO had contemplated this for weeks. He held numerous meetings about it. He had executives who were supportive of the acquisition as well as executives who were against it.

The CEO was against the acquisition. He believed that an acquisition may appear favorable in the short term to please investors, but could present problems in the long term for the company. The CEO called a meeting with an external business advisor.

The advisor came to the CEO's office and listened to the CEO describe the situation and the different stakes in the decision. The CEO said that he believed the best decision would be to continue operating without an acquisition.

The business advisor said, "I agree with your decision," and left.

The next day, the CEO received an invoice for $20,000 from the business advisor. The CEO's assistant was incredulous.

"But he was in your office for less than 15 minutes!" The assistant said.

The CEO said, "Pay the invoice. The $20,000 probably saved me hundreds of millions of dollars."

There are many people who thought like the assistant: they looked at units as what was important to count. They counted hours worked as proof of productivity. They counted number of pages in a book as proof of knowledge. They counted pieces of information as proof of insight.

On the other hand, the CEO knew that he was not paying for units of time, but for insight that could only come through depth and breadth of industry experience. This is why the CEO sits in his position as a chief executive. He has probably learned lessons many ways including the least time efficient and costly ways. In his current position, he cannot afford to learn by trial and error – now, his own job is not the only job at stake.

Information is cheap. You can get information at low cost or free through the internet connection. On the other hand, insight demands a premium because insight is not readily accessible or is hidden in plain sight. Insight matters only to the person who needs it. Whether you are a job seeker or CEO, differentiating information from insight is critical to your success.

Insight comes from information that has been analyzed, digested, and transformed to be actionable and specifically, for making decisions.

Insight can come from industry insiders or outsiders, but insight becomes actionable only when a person who needs it can recognize it and knows how to use it. When it comes to career transitioning, **the lack of insight (or perceived lack of insight) is part of the "under-experienced" objection** you may hear. This is because insight is not a skill that is taught. You have to gain it through experience. Thus, insight is an aspect of experience gained through the job that employers are looking for.

When I used to coach aspiring medical science liaisons, I shortened their learning curve by providing them with insight they otherwise would have to invest a lot of resources to acquire, if they had never worked as a MSL. My insight came from being an industry insider and having worked with MSL employers as a consultant.

I knew what was in employers' minds and what they worried about when hiring people. I knew what questions they asked themselves when evaluating candidates. I knew what would make them take risks to hire a person without prior MSL experience when they could just as easily hire an applicant with MSL experience.

My insight is part of what clients paid for – not information. If they wanted information, they could root through the internet for the cost of their internet connection. Another part of what clients pay me for, is the time they save by not having to generate the same level of insight for themselves. They can spend the time needed to gather all the information, analyze the information to distill insight – or they can tap into the source of insight and save time. In business, time costs money. Spending a lot of time to save a bit of money can cost a business even more money in the long run.

Employers can tell the difference between job applicants who had simply read about the career versus those job applicants who knew the career beyond what is superficially offered. Employers are experts at their own hiring preferences and write the job descriptions they are hiring for. They are more likely to interview applicants who have demonstrated in-depth knowledge and insight about the job even if that person has not yet done the job.

How Employers Evaluate "Experience"

When employers talk about experience, they are evaluating whether you:

- Know the system/industry.

- Speak the language of the system/industry.

- Can work with others in the system/industry.

- Can produce results for the system/industry.

Employers rarely evaluate experience in isolation; they are looking specifically to hire people who can do the job and who fit into their company culture. Culture is a product of the system, which is made up of people, property (physical and intellectual), and process. You can have the right kind of job experience but if you don't look like you'd be the right fit for the company culture, you would still not be hired for the job.

Know the System

Do you know how basic businesses operate? If you do, then you are a step ahead of your competitors who don't. If you don't, then now is the time to learn. The system has physical, logistical, and hierarchical structures. The physical and logistical structures are related ideas: the physical location of a company can dictate how that company can operate logistically.

Does the company have branch offices? Are employees primarily located "in-house", coming to work in their offices during the week? Are there significant numbers of employees who are field-based, working from their home office? A company that is located in Manhattan, New York has a different logistical profile from a company that is located in downtown Los Angeles, California. Even the way employees get to work at each metropolitan subsidiary would be different.

Logistical traits will influence how those employees communicate what they are doing on the company's behalf, how often they may spend commuting or traveling, and even affect their career advancement strategies. A system's hierarchical structure or its organizational chart ("org. chart") describes the layers and ranks of its human resources ("people", employees). An org. chart can look like this:

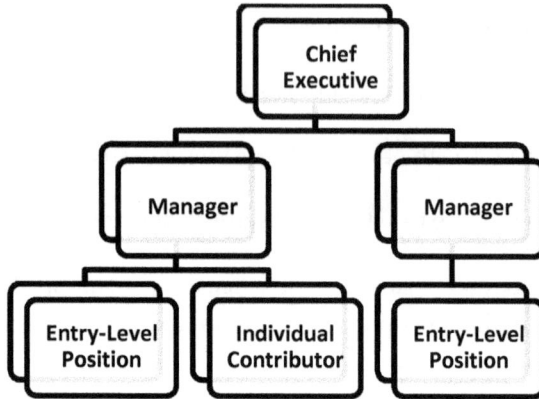

```
                    ┌─────────────┐
                    │   Chief     │
                    │  Executive  │
                    └─────────────┘
            ┌───────────┴───────────┐
      ┌───────────┐           ┌───────────┐
      │  Manager  │           │  Manager  │
      └───────────┘           └───────────┘
      ┌─────┴─────┐                 │
┌────────────┐ ┌────────────┐ ┌────────────┐
│ Entry-Level│ │ Individual │ │ Entry-Level│
│  Position  │ │ Contributor│ │  Position  │
└────────────┘ └────────────┘ └────────────┘
```

At the foundational level of a business are individual contributors and entry-level employees. These employees are sometimes called rank-and-file employees. Entry-level employees may include those responsible for janitorial and maintenance of the facilities to customer service representative, sales agents, or manufacturing personnel.

These positions tend to pay the least of all positions within a company, but not always. You may find someone who earns more at these positions than someone in middle management. This is especially true of jobs of highly technical or specialized individual contributors. For example, an experienced aerospace engineer can be an individual contributor who has no formal subordinates ("direct reports") and still command a substantive salary (over U.S. $100,000 per year) based on technical expertise.

Management makes up the layers between the chief executives and individual contributors in the organization. The larger the organization, the more layers of management you will have.

This is where you begin to see different titles for management and a distinction between middle management and upper management. For example, vice presidents of companies are considered upper management. Associate directors and directors may belong to middle management.

As a general rule, the closer to the chief executive a management job title appears the more likely that position is upper management. The closer to the individual contributor a management job title appears, the more likely that position belongs to middle management.

Why should you care about understanding organizational hierarchy?

First, you want to show that you understand the system so that when you speak with prospective employers, you demonstrate your knowledge of the system. But an equally important reason to knowing the system is so that you will know where you want to start looking for jobs! The problem with typical organizational charts is that most people assume that entry-level positions exist only at the foundational layers or ground-levels of the hierarchy.

Entry-level positions at companies aren't geared toward PhD-holding professionals, because those positions are designed as training positions for people who have at most a bachelor's degree and are looking to get into the company at the ground-level.

These positions are expected to have a high turnover, making it very inefficient for companies to hire and train new people unless the salaries for these employees reflect this entry-level status. The company can then control costs of high turnover by paying a lower wage for these positions.

PhD applicants looking for a first career within a corporation may look for individual contributor positions that are specialized or highly technical positions, but hierarchically are located downstream of management positions but are upstream of, or lateral to, entry-level positions.

These are the types of positions geared toward individuals with specialized training and advanced degrees, which means you will have a better chance of being considered with your PhD degree even if you have never worked in that job before.

You now have the challenge of uncovering these positions, because these job postings may be hidden in plain sight through the language of the system: jargon.

Speak the Language of the System

If you earned a PhD degree in economics and you had never heard of the term, "pharmaceutical outcomes", then you could see hundreds of these job postings and have no idea that these jobs mean, or whether you may have a good chance of being considered as an applicant.

This is because companies use monikers and terms that are known readily to industry insiders who know the language of the system but are obscure to outsiders not familiar with the system. Jargon acts as first-pass filtration for companies to funnel out applicants who are not familiar with the system.

Learning the language of the system allows you to communicate with employers on their own terms and in their familiar language. This is an important aspect in building rapport and establishing credibility so that employers who are ready to step outside of their comfort zone to hire a PhD professional will look at your application seriously.

Learning the language of the system allows you to be seen. Many employers find PhD applicants difficult to evaluate in first-pass screening processes because most of them don't understand the jargon on PhDs' resumes.

PhDs can convert their academic curriculum vitae or CV into a resume, which makes their resume a shorter version of their CV, but this remains undecipherable and incomprehensible to employers. PhD resumes are full of esoteric jargon familiar to a specialized department within an academic employment system. Then the employers say, "He does not appear ready to leave academia," because that was the message the resume was sending to employers by its jargon.

The language of the system is made up of terms specific to and known by system insiders. This includes acronyms that people native to the system are familiar with.

For example, if you want to work in the social media industry, you would know what the acronym SEO stands for, you will know the difference between "white hat" from "black hat" strategies, and you'd probably be conversant about user experience, cloud-sourcing, and web analytics. If I drop you into the middle of a crowd of social media professionals at a conference and you open your mouth to speak, I shouldn't see the crowd clearing away from you because they can't relate to what you are saying. Instead, they will gather around you, an industry "outsider" with an understanding of their system, and look for fresh ways of looking at age-old problems.

One way to acquire the language of the system is through immersion:

- You read articles and trade journals about the system or published for/by the system.

- You find people who are insiders to the system – constituents (people working in the system) and consultants (people doing business with the system).

- You create a value proposition so that industry insiders will be willing to speak with you about the system.

- You may offer to hire them as coaches and mentors to shorten your learning curve. You attend conferences that people in the system attend.

- You subscribe to magazines and journals people in the system write for.

Immersion is what enables a person to pick up a foreign language and become fluent in a short period of time. Immersion also costs time and money; not everyone will be willing to make this level of investment. This is why those who are willing to invest at this level can give their career a competitive advantage over those who aren't willing to immerse when competing for the same jobs.

Practical Application: Identify 10-20 words that are part of the language of the system, or "jargon" including acronyms. In the MSL world, for example, a jargon would be "key opinion leader" and "thought leader." In the regulatory world, a jargon would be "NDA", "Preclinical", "Post-marketing studies/surveillance."

Work With Others in the System

PhDs competing for work outside academia can face stereotypes and biases about their personalities. Some of these stereotypes and biases have truth in them, and these kernels of truth about academic PhDs may be the very reason why you as a PhD no longer want to work within academia. Unfortunately, many non-academic employers may hold the same stereotype and prejudices against *you*, the PhD job seeker.

Employers worry about disruption to a team environment when hiring a person whose degree may create dissent or fear from existing employees. For example, when employers begin to hire candidates with advanced degrees to their teams, existing non-PhD team members may feel threatened. The incoming team members with advanced degrees may be suspected as "here to replace me". This causes strain in existing work relationships.

Now let's take this scenario and build forward: when an employer staffs a research department with both PhD-trained and masters-trained scientists, there is sensitivity about "who gets promoted to management before whom." I worked at a company where the masters-trained scientists complained that PhD-trained scientists had more advancement opportunities to management while masters-trained scientists did not have the same opportunities even when MS scientists viewed themselves as capable managers.

Employers may worry about the different communication culture of a PhD applicant who comes from academia. It may be normal for a group of PhD scientists to have a rigorous debate about one of their members' project ideas, and have no second thought about making statements like, "This hypothesis is completely ridiculous!" However, outside the academic world, you will be working with people who have not been exposed to this type of academic jousting. They will interpret the same statement as being called "stupid" by a colleague.

One of the employers I spoke with when researching this book said that he once hired a PhD who did not have much social tact when giving criticism to peers and subordinates. The employer then had to spend time in damage control mode, mending relationships between his employees and working through what some of his team members saw as personal attacks by the PhD team member. The employer admits subsequently shying away from hiring PhDs because he does not want to spend most of his time dealing with "HR (human resource) issues."

You can say that you are a people-person. You can tell employers how much you love working with people. This isn't enough: your competitors are saying the same things. Your exposure to multi-disciplinary, cross-departmental collaboration can be a critical point of differentiation for you as a PhD job seeker.

You can show prospective employers that you work well with people in your familiar system like your department or lab, but this is not very persuasive to non-academic employers as a demonstration of people skills (plus, academics do not have a reputation of having great people skills with non-academic employers). Instead, show employers how you have been successful in creating new work relationships with a different department or with very different groups of people than the ones you are most familiar with. *Showing* employers how you have been effective with different groups of people will differentiate you from competitors who can only *tell* employers that they like working with people.

Practical Application: Give 3-5 specific examples of how you have "worked" with people, including scenarios where:

You had to get different mindsets on board with a project or idea;

You had to bridge different personalities and communication styles;

You had to manage a conflict within the project team;

You had to manage unrealistic expectations about the project results or timeline for delivery;

You may draw from your current experience working with your department, but don't limit yourself to only academic work experience. Feel free to use examples from your community activities or non-academic leadership activities. This is where engaging in extracurricular activities can benefit and enhance your job seeker profile.

Produce Results for the System

Take a look at your resume right now. Have you simply regurgitated job descriptions on your resumes? If the answer is yes, start over. Employers read resume after resume brimming with job descriptions that told only what the applicants were supposed to do, but showed little or nothing of what the applicants had actually done on the job.

Think of your resume as a collection of the most memorable accomplishments or the most tangible ways you had made a difference through your work. Find a way to provide the most robust level of evidence that you can provide when demonstrating your contribution as employee.

Yes, you HAVE experience! Unless you had been hiding under a rock instead of completing your research projects or doing the work you had agreed to do for your adviser, you accomplished *something*. This should be true whether you were a PhD student, a postdoctoral researcher, or a junior faculty member. The issue is that this *something* may not be comprehensible to employers outside the academic walls. You would need to translate what you had accomplished into a universal language, an *objective means* for all employers could understand without having to work in your field.

Here are major categories that you could translate your accomplishments from an academic resume into one that is readily understandable by employers, especially those in an applied-field or business world:

- Time saved

- Manpower saved

- Money saved

- Money made

- Applied Innovation

This is a general list, but anything that would increase or improve the *potential* for any of the above could be used as evidence demonstrating your readiness to produce results for an employer. For example, if you had created a process that reduced human error, this could potentially save time and money, especially money relating to liability resulting from error. If you published papers that were cited a number of times, you may view this as applied innovation where others built upon your work to advance their hypotheses. Showing the influence of your work is more compelling to alternative career employers than sharing what your work entailed.

To translate your current academic CV into one that uses objective, universal metrics, you need to get comfortable with *numbers*. Employers remember numbers, especially numbers that relate to money/time saved or money made. Let's look at an example of two versions describing a typical job description of a junior-level faculty member at a large university. In version A below, the PhD professional had written his resume in the typical format of "what he did" on the job.

Version A

- Developed an independent research program.

- Taught undergraduate, graduate, and professional students.

The language was not complicated, so even if you weren't an academic professional, you could understand what the candidate had done. The problem is, understanding what the candidate has done does not make the candidate particularly memorable. You may also question how these skills could transfer to a non-academic world. What if, instead of Version A, you read this version?

Version B

- Developed a $585,000 new research program 3 months ahead of schedule and created 2 new operating procedures that improved laboratory efficiency by 35% while reducing human resource errors by 15%.

- Consistently delivered 85%-95% satisfaction scores as instructor to over 900 students each semester for the past 5 semesters.

Employers don't have to understand what your exact job is at the university and they will all understand what you had accomplished in Version B.

They will see an applicant who understood the cost of operating an enterprise – whether this was a corporate enterprise or an academic enterprise. They will see an applicant who tracked his own performance against customer expectations and therefore someone who understood the importance of customers, no matter whether the customers were students, consumers (in business-to-consumer or B2C sales) or businesses (in business-to-business or B2B sales).

When employers see numbers like these on a PhD applicant's resume, they will be more receptive to the possibility that this PhD applicant is transition-ready for a non-academic job. Learn to view objective variables like time, manpower, and innovation as a function of money saved/money made. When you save time, you save money. When you increase the effectiveness or efficiency in manpower, you save money and make money, or at least, improve current earnings. When you innovate, you can save time, money, and manpower, as well as increase potential to earn money in new markets.

Learn to write your resumes using these functional relationships and your resume will immediately become understandable and more memorable to employers. Your resume will stand ahead of resumes that streamed lists of job descriptions. One PhD I worked with took the time to find these numbers in his research track record. When he released his resume into the job application pool, he was pleasantly surprised to get queries from employers in functional areas of industry that he was not even prospecting.

Employers understand numbers and results. Employers look for employees who also understand numbers and results to the degree that is appropriate for the position. The higher the position resides at an organization, the more critical numbers and results become. If you have ambitions to advance to the executive ranks of organizations, now is the time to learn how to think in numbers even when you deal with mostly qualitative work, as most knowledge work tend to be. Employers want employees who had shown a verifiable track record of delivering results in their respective careers.

What You Can Do

Go through your resume and start looking for the numbers that matter. It may not be an easy exercise if you are not used to looking at your accomplishments this way, but this will be time well-spent, and go a long way to overcoming the under-experienced objection.

If you're reading this book, then you probably do your homework and perform due diligence about the career that you are very serious about entering. You have probably talked to as many people as you can find willing to talk with you about the career.

You have probably attended networking receptions and gone to as many industry conferences as you could afford on your meager salary. You have probably paid your own way to workshops that you hope to give you an advantage over your competition in the job market.

Let's pretend that I was the employer. You had impressed me so much during the face-to-face interview that at the end of the interview, I extended my hand to you and said, "Congratulations, you're hired! Sign this contract... good. You start right now."

How would you start? Where would you start? What would you do? I'm not talking about the part where you sign an array of legal documents that make you official as an employee. I'm talking about the specific actions you will take within the first 30 days of your employment that should make me, your employer, look at your personnel file and say, "They all told me that I was taking a big risk, but now I can show them that I was right in hiring him!"

Don't have experience? You have to go get some. I'm not trying to be funny. If you worried that you didn't have enough experience to apply for the job that you wanted, then find a way to replicate that experience through alternative approaches.

One of my friends is a former pharmaceutical sales executive who wrote a book on getting a career in pharmaceutical sales. He recommended people who were serious about pharmaceutical sales to do thorough research – about the company, about the products, about the career itself – and about the customers.

The main responsibility of this sales position is interacting with ("calling on") doctors. If a person did not have pharmaceutical sales experience and wanted to show how serious he as about working in pharmaceutical sales, then this manager expected the candidate to speak with as many doctors as the candidate could gain access to.

He expected the candidates to do their homework even before the interview and ask doctors what they expected from reps and what would make a sales rep stand above his peers from other reps that the doctors saw on a daily basis. If the candidate was too uncomfortable to approach doctors' offices and ask these questions or if the candidate deemed this exercise premature or worse, beneath him – then that person was not suited for a pharmaceutical sales job, where facing rejection was part of the daily routine.

For example, a member who belonged to the social networking group I had created for PhDs interested in alternative careers was a 4th year graduate student majoring in molecular biology. She had set her eyes on a career in science policy. While this graduate student worked in the lab, she enriched her non-research professional experience with activities outside lab research. These activities would help her develop critical skills that would be relevant to her career aspiration.

She joined specific student activity groups to gain skills in lobbying, advertising, and teamwork. She took courses in science policy. She signed up for committees to learn how departmental decisions are made. Even though graduate student had a supervisor who discouraged her from exploring non-academic career options and she had to conduct these activities "in secret, at night, and on weekends", she was not deterred in her effort to gain transferable experience.

By the time she graduated with her doctorate degree, she would also have a wealth of transferable experience to show prospective employers.

Even if you don't succeed in replicating the results as if you are already employed in your dream job, prospective employers will be impressed that you have done more than just promise your potential: you have taken concrete actions to demonstrate your willingness to turn your potential into performance. And you'll have more memorable stories to tell during the job interview!

Your turn:

- Write out your 30-60-90 day plan if you had just received an offer for your dream job. Who will your customers or stakeholders be? What will your employer expect you to accomplish by the end of month 1, 2, and 3?

- Brainstorm a list of how you think your employer will evaluate your performance in your dream job: is it based on the number of people you interact with? How many articles you write? How many customers you convert? How much a satisfaction score has improved? How much more efficient is a process or a system?

- Imagine that your employer comes up to you and said, "you have done an excellent job, keep this up and you'll advance quickly!" What have you accomplished and done to get this kind of feedback?

- Based on your 30-60-90 day plan, what activities can you do or start right now to get the skills you will need to successfully accomplish the goals you have set for yourself?

∞

7. PHD CAREER PROFESSIONAL, KNOW THYSELF

What you are about to read in this chapter is what sparked this book. It was September 2010, more than 3 years since I had offered a limited release of my workbook, *5 Lessons in PhD Career Transitions*. I was active in an online group for PhDs interested in careers outside academia. I read and answered questions from PhDs aspiring toward viable career alternatives to academic research and faculty positions.

I felt as if I was answering the same types of questions again and again. The frustrations sounded familiar, the struggles eerily similar no matter how different the PhDs' fields of study were. But I couldn't say that I was surprised at the questions I'd read, because I had many of the same questions when I was in graduate school and wondering what I was going to do next.

I began typing up a list: a list of lessons that I wished PhDs didn't have to learn the hard way, through costly mistakes and precious time wasted, on route to a career outside academia. The first half of the list became the first chapters of this book. These chapters dealt with cultivating mental toughness when enduring the harshness of a career transition that may still be stigmatized in academic circles, growing your social network that supplied the referrals and opportunities for your career future, and confronting the myths of being overqualified and under-experienced.

The second half of the list were lessons that could influence how successful you became once you had made that leap into the unknown. This second half of the list was what could help you accelerate your career success outside academia, and it was all about awareness: from awareness of "the big picture" to organizational awareness to self-awareness. This chapter covers that second half of the list.

Self-awareness – or knowing thyself – sounds like a soft skill that should be better served by therapists or philosophy classes. Yet I see self-awareness as a hardcore business aptitude for anyone who is interested in a career move to non-traditional realms.

This is because your talents and motivations are the instruments with which you will create viable alternative futures. Therefore, you must gain mastery of how to use these instruments, and the first step is to know what these instruments are. When you leap into a different career, your motives and mental models will be questioned by employers skeptical about your knowledge of "what you are getting yourself into."

One way to efficient self-discovery is through assessments that identify your personality style and decision-making style. You may be able to find free online versions of personality assessments such as the Myers Briggs test, but you will need to find certified practitioners or specialists who are qualified to provide and interpret other types of assessments.

For example, the Herrmann Brain Dominance Instrument is a fee-based assessment that is administered by a certified practitioner. This instrument is not cheap but it shows dominant thinking styles and particularly how stressful situations can cause you to rely on certain thinking style that can be counterproductive. One useful piece of information I gained through the HBDI instrument is what tends to happen when I'm under stress: the assessment suggests that I will become even more analytical than I already am. This is my way of creating artificial controls over my environment. By becoming even more analytical, I may be able to organize my thoughts and manage feelings of stress, but this may come at the expense of creative thinking that can lead to novel solutions to the problem that has caused the stressful situation.

A cost-effective way to gain access to fee-based assessments is to visit your university's career center, either as a current student or alumnus. Universities can get institutional rates for assessments and offer them free to students and alumni. Many independent career consultants or life coaches are certified to provide assessments of your strengths and thinking or relating styles.

Separate Roles from Identity
When I took a professional development program through Sandler Training (created by the late David H. Sandler), one of the first concepts I learned was to differentiate "roles" from "identity". I can hold many roles in life – entrepreneur, wife, friend, mother, and author – but I have one

identity. I can score how I feel about my role versus my identity differently on any given day.

For example, if I had made a calculated business risk that didn't work out, I may feel poorly about my role as an entrepreneur based on that outcome. I would give myself score a score of 5 on a scale of 1 to 10 for effectiveness in an entrepreneurial role. However, I could still score myself a 9 or a 10 for my feeling about my identity.

This seems like a trivial exercise, but when you take an emotional risk of any kind – changing careers, making a new friend, learning a new skill – you may find keeping these scores a useful tool to maintain a healthy perspective about you.

David Sandler introduced this scoring early on in the sales training program because sales people face rejection every single day. Sales people cannot afford to let a rude customer or a failed sale devastate their feelings of self-worth, or they will not be able to get out of the bed the next morning and start the process all over again.

By separating roles from identity, we learn to separate the mistakes we will inevitably make through the many roles we can play from the intrinsic worth of who we are as people. This is important in developing emotional resilience.

If we see each failure as corrosive to our self-worth, it becomes harder for us to try something new the next time, in case we fail again or make more mistakes. We will avoid taking new risks because we won't want to fail. We may even avoid excellence, for those of us who fear success.

But if we see each failure as part of the learning process for one of many roles we hold through life, we will be better prepared to draw upon our internal reserve of strength (from our identity) and suffer through the spectrum of emotions we will experience every time we fail or make mistakes. We will be more willing to get through feelings of disappointment, anger, embarrassment, grief, and fear when we err or fail. We can recover from pain, learn the lessons, identify our blindspots, and try again.

Answer Your Big Questions

Most of the big decisions that I have made come from careful deliberation of big questions that I have asked myself.

I will admit that I didn't always ask these important questions, especially early in my career. As a result, I traveled my career path haphazardly, and it was because I have learned to grow my luck that I buffered my career against decisions that I had made unconsciously.

What you are looking to do through these big questions is find out what your *core values* are in life. These values are ones that, if you compromise them or lose them, will guarantee your emotional implosion and decline. You will literally wither and die from the inside.

Why do some people who seem to have it all do something stupid to jeopardize what they hold precious to them? Why do some people who should be happy with all that they have never seem to feel happy? Then there are those people who look like they have lost it all – why are some of them able to rise above their circumstances? The answer is found in *the level of congruency between how they lived and what they had defined as their core values in life based on their answers to the list of big questions.*

Here is my list of big questions:

1. What/who do I care deeply about?

2. Why do I care deeply about {my answer to previous question}?

3. What am I willing to do about what I care deeply about?

4. How far am I willing to go/persevere/sacrifice for this?

5. How prepared am I to suffer the consequences, not just reap the rewards, for this decision?

6. How willing am I to expose my loved ones to these consequences of my actions?

7. At what point would I give up/change course/change my mind? [Please keep in mind that you also have the option to say "never" to changing course or giving up or changing your mind.]

People who self-sabotage are those who are not making decisions based on what they have said to be important to their values.

Question 6 looks like it reiterates questions 1 and 2, but this question is nuanced. I have met people who made decisions that had risked the integrity of sanctity of their relationships with the people they said they care about, yet they may not have been willing to take such a risk if they had first defined how much they were willing to risk. By defining up-front how far you are willing to go to expose risk to the relationships that matter to you, you can make decisions with a higher degree of self-awareness and responsibility.

When we are under pressure and demanded to make decisions, having our value-definitions from doing our big questions exercise can safeguard us from making mistakes we will later regret.

Take time and answer these questions for yourself, so that you can make your major career and life transitions with both eyes open.

Get Clear about Self-Confidence
Some people seemed to be born with a lot of self-confidence.

I am not one of those people.

Because I am very self-critical, I have to work at gaining self-confidence and focus on what I need to do instead of doubting whether I am doing it perfectly.

What I have found is that if my confidence relies too much on the opinions of other people, when people's opinions change or are based on incomplete or incorrect information about me, my confidence suffers. Therefore, my confidence needs to be based on variables that are within my control.

First, I identified qualities within myself that I hold in high esteem and get specific about how I uniquely express these qualities. These qualities are what I consider as important traits for me to have as a person.

I hold in high esteem qualities of compassion, empathy, creativity, critical thinking. But this is only part of the equation. I also need to get very clear about how I uniquely express each of the qualities that I hold in high esteem. This is crucial, because words like "compassion, empathy, creativity" are general and can hold different meanings to different people. Therefore, this step aims to have you clarify how you express a quality in your own special way.

I express my creativity by using stories or lessons learned to help people avoid mistakes. I use critical thinking to help people see many angles of the same situation, so they can make better decisions. This is more specific and clear than saying "I am a creative person." Being specific lets me identify what I can do that is within my control to reinforce, and therefore build self-confidence.

Second, I identify actions that signal an increase in self-confidence. I used to be one of those people who thought never asking for help was a sign of strength and confidence, when in reality; it was my fear of having to depend on someone and risk being disappointed or betrayed. As I began to identify that a signal of self-confidence was being able to ask for help when I needed help, I became aware of specific actions I could take to reaffirm my self-confidence.

Another signal that I have identified is to say "Yes" to doing something new and scary (usually because I have never done it before). This is part of taking emotional risks where I may make a mistake or fail. Regardless of outcome, I will have gained a new experience that increases my self-confidence. I can at least say, "I've done this. It didn't work out so well, but I did it."

Third, I surround myself with supportive people. You can do the first two steps of this exercise, but if you surround yourself with people who constantly put you down or find everything they can find wrong with you, then you undermine your efforts in building self-confidence.

This is not a call for you to surround yourself with fawning fans and sycophants. This is about surrounding yourself with people who are supportive of what you are trying to do, and who can make you feel safe when you are risking. You can feel safe admitting you have made a mistake without being criticized or judged.

You are perfectly within your right to fire and otherwise disown people who can't stop putting you down or otherwise hold you in contempt for any reason.

Manage Your Blind Spots

Blindspots can be hazardous to your career, because you are not aware that you have a blind spot until the consequences of this blind spot hit you in the face. This is just like driving your car and not turning your head to see if there is another vehicle approaching before you changed lanes. If you had turned into the lane, you would have hit the car that you didn't see.

If something was truly a blind spot, you will not know what you do not know. But you can practice palpating where you blind spots hide, just as you know to watch out for blind spots when driving. One useful way to palpate your blind spots is to ask people you trust.

Practical Application: Choose 3-5 people you can trust with this exercise. Ask them, "In the past when I have made mistakes that I could have otherwise avoided, what do you think I may have missed seeing?"

You may be surprised with what answers you glean from people who have observed you and know you well.

Our personal blind spots are formed by assumptions and habits. In business, blind spots can form when people see a problem but are unwilling to openly discuss the problem or were instructed against talking about the problem. These problems perpetuate and infiltrate company culture to become a subculture or shadow culture that wields tremendous control over the health of the organization.

Think of the fairy tale about the Emperor's Clothes and you get a taste of what blind spots may look like: obvious to others but oblivious to the one with the blind spot.

In business, this lulls executives into believing that they are secure in their market leadership when, in fact, competitors have been overtaking them or changing the rules of the market for months.

Our personal blind spots can come through cultural conditioning that colors our thinking process, beliefs, and quick mental check-lists that we use to make life feasible and functional. Often, these conditions meet our objectives and serve us well. Occasionally, outliers and exceptions to the rule change what we usually would expect to happen. If we do not ask that extra question or pause for that extra second before reacting, we will have fallen prey to our habit and conditioning – our blind spots.

Throughout the book, I used different methods of removing specific blinders that could keep you from moving forward in your transition to an alternative career option. You can also engage people that you trust to help uncover your blind spots. Find people who have different career experiences and life experiences and skills than you have. They can offer you a very different perspective to the same situation, and point out solutions that you may not immediately see.

∞

8. PUTTING IT ALL TOGETHER: DEVELOP YOUR CAREER STRATEGIC PLAN

This chapter is a template for your career strategic plan. Use it!

Vision

Your career vision statement describes **where you want to be** in your career path. Develop your career vision statement using specific time frames and levels of involvement for activities or projects, NOT job titles.

Whenever I ask PhDs where they want to be, they pull out nouns (job titles) instead of giving me verbs (activities or constellation of activities as projects). The reason why I stay away from job titles is because this immediately limits your creativity when this is a "visioning" portion of your career strategic plan and therefore, requests your creativity.

Your vision should remain value-based and based on "the big picture" of your talent contribution to the world, regardless of industry or market.

For example, "In 3-5 years, I want to be known as the professional who:

- People call FIRST to solve Problem X

- People rely on for insight to Industry Y

- Is known for being a Valuable (Role) Z

Describe X, Y, and Z as part of your visioning exercise.

Next, distill the "essence" of X, Y, and Z into words or vivid description of how you will be known as a professional.

My words are "Thought Leader" and "Catalyst". I can think of people whose words / vivid description include "Connection Agent", "Person who turns toxic teams into cooperative, productive employees", and "Contrarian".

You want to be known as:

_____

Mission Statement

Your career mission statement takes your vision statement and describes **how you will get to where you want to be**. What are some of the goals you must set for yourself to realize the career vision you have set for yourself? What are specific actions you will take to achieve these goals?

To use my own example: "I will become a thought leader-catalyst in my industry by *writing, speaking, and advising* in the chosen topics of my industry. I will engage in a particular style of *learning* that will support my vision as thought leader-catalyst."

Here is how I'd describe my career vision, mission, and goals (we will cover goals & objectives later in this chapter):

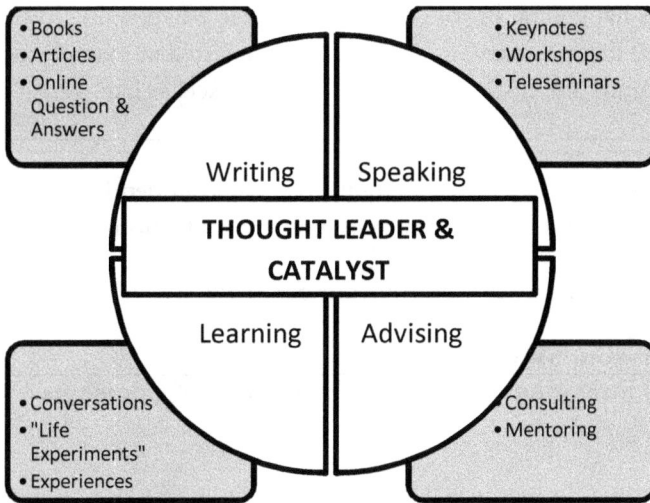

You can be creative or use a simple document to describe your career vision-mission relationship. What is important is that you describe your vision and mission in whatever form you prefer to describe it.

Your mission statement:
_____
_____
_____

SWOT Analysis

Next, you will conduct a SWOT (Strengths, Weaknesses, Opportunities, Threats) analysis of your current status as a professional within a given industry/job market.

(Your) Strengths	**(Your) Weaknesses**
What are your strengths as a professional in your current industry? What are your current assets (relationships, insight)?	What are your weaknesses as a professional in your chosen industry? A possible weakness: "overqualified/under-experienced"
(Market) Opportunities	**(Market) Threats**
What is happening in your chosen industry that presents an opportunity for you?	What is happening in your chosen industry that may present threats to a job seeker like you?

Opportunities and Threats require you to do in-depth research, including information interviews of current industry professionals.

Don't skimp on "in-depth": your competitive advantage depends on it.

Fill out your SWOT:

(Your) Strengths	**(Your) Weaknesses**
(Market) Opportunities	**(Market) Threats**

Goals and Objectives

Based on your mission statement, identify the goals you must set to fulfill your mission. Once you have identified your goals, create a list of time-bound objectives that you must meet to achieve your goals.

For example, if I want to create a presence for myself as *"thought leader"* (vision) through *writing* (mission) at an *online Q&A website* (goal), then my *objectives* may be the specific web venues I want to participate/write in. For me, this may be LinkedIn, Quora, and Twitter (Twitter is not quite Q&A).

Action Plans

Use the template below or come up with your own action plan "tracking sheet". You can recreate this with a spreadsheet application:

Goal: _____				
Objectives	**Task/Action**	**Due Date**	**Resources Needed**	**Outcome**

Task/Action is what you will do by what date (*Due Date*).

Resources Needed help you identify "what" or "who" are necessary part of your ability to carry through the action.

Metrics is the result or outcome you will track, and can be as simple as a check mark "Accepted" or "50% Done" or even "Tabled/Canceled".

Evaluation of Career Strategy Plan

If you are growing along your career path and you have a personal life, you will probably need to evaluate and modify your career strategy plan according to your growth curve and life transition. Some common life transitions include a change in marital status, becoming a parent, or being a primary caretaker of a dependent (such as aging parents or an elderly relative). Other uncommon, but possible life transitions may include becoming disabled or suffering a chronic health issue.

Periodically evaluate your career strategy plan, especially its relevance based on your growth as a professional:

- Is my vision still valid?

- Has my mission changed?

- Is my SWOT relevant and correct?

- Are my goals appropriate? Should I add more goals? Should I delete some of these goals?

- Do the objectives need updating? [This is especially critical if you start executing on your action plans and you keep hitting roadblocks and obstacles. You may need to evaluate your approach whether this is at the objectives level or the goals level.]

- Do I need to acquire specific skills? [You may identify gaps in your skills that are preventing you from executing on an objective. Typical skills gap may include Communication skills and Negotiation skills. You may then need to create an objective around acquiring those skills as a priority.]

Once you become familiar with your career strategy plan, you can adapt and modify the format and remain effective and on track. One year, my strategy plan consists of a stack of 3X5 index (note) cards, each labeled with a "project code name" on one side, and a list of objectives on the other side. This book, for example, was on one of those index cards.

∞

APPENDIX: MATRIX METHOD APPLICATION PROCESS FOR PHD JOB SEEKERS

This career tool is provided by **Lawrence Arnold**, Director of Career Counseling Melbourne, and a member of our Alternative PhD Careers group on LinkedIn.

This tool is for your eyes only: do not give it to the recruiter or employer.

The 8 workplace skills used in these exercises are:

- communication

- team work

- problem solving

- initiative and enterprise

- planning and organizing at the wider organizational level

- self-management

- ongoing learning

- use of technology

For any job description you should find requirements for many or all of these workplace skills, whether these requirements are explicitly required or implicitly expected.

Recruiter and hiring managers have templates for determining your suitability for the position; in other words they are building their own "matrices" of you as an employment candidate.

Use a blank sheet of paper for creating and populating these matrices.

Contact employer or recruiter to discuss position description. *Research employer or sector for key business directions.* **My information sources:**	*Present your strengths through the process.* **Where my strengths appear:**	*Differentiate yourself through your internships or work history.* **My differences:**
Address selection criteria separately in application or in cover letter. **All covered?**	*Integrate position duties or selection criteria into cover letter.* **Decision on which to include:**	*Integrate selection criteria into your CV skills summary.* **Changes to CV:**
Which of the 8 workplace skills will you highlight?	**Prepare 8 employability skills document for interview:**	*Give referees your application or key selection criteria.* **Why choose these referees?**

Recruiter's Perspective

"Best fit" is a function of how well your matrix aligns with the recruiters' or hiring managers' matrix.

Has the applicant used multiple entry points to find out about us, our needs and the position? This shows real interest in the position, the business and the industry.	*Are there any personal negatives? Will the person fit in?*	*Is the applicant similar to other applicants or are there some special aspects that the organization can use?*
Can we check all selection criteria in the application?	*Can the person do the job?* ■ skills ■ qualifications ■ experience	*Will the applicant need any special professional development or support?*
Will the person do the job? ■ enthusiasm ■ attitudes	*Does everything fit, or are there discrepancies or mysteries we don't have an answer for?*	*Are the applicant's references able to give us the information we need to make a decision?*

Skills Matrix

List the position's key responsibilities outlined in the job description or discovered through your investigation.

Identify the necessary skills and list the evidence highlighting these skills from past educational and professional experience. Use bullet points for the purpose of this exercise.

Responsibilities	Your Skills	Evidence

The STAR Method of Answering Questions

Some online application forms require you to answer questions as part of your application process. The STAR acronym is a structured method of answering questions including interview questions.

Start with a sentence like, *'I have shown a high level of initiative (or teamwork, flexibility, or communication skills with clients etc.) throughout my previous positions and internships.'*

Then follow the STAR response structure:

Situation: Briefly describe the situation of your choice. Give just enough information to set the scene for the employer. Cut out unnecessary details. This shows capacity for awareness.

'When I was working as a ….. in the ….. there was a situation that came up in which ……'

Task: Say what you thought the problem or issue was. A lot of the books and websites omit this step. Don't leave it out as, if there was no problem, why were you taking action? This shows capacity for analysis.

'When I appraised the situation I realized that the task was to …….'

Action: Say what action you personally took. There may have been others who contributed to the solution as well. You can mention that but concentrate on what you actually did. This shows capacity for judgment and follow-through.

'The action I took was to ……… This seemed to be working so I continued to …… and then informed my supervisor' or *'That action didn't seem to be working so I decided to ……. instead'*

Result: Say what the result was. *'The result of the action I took was ……'*

This shows capacity for evaluation.

The result should have been basically successful or at least have improved the situation. It doesn't have to be 100% successful every time. If it wasn't totally successful, this gives you a chance to show how you would change your actions the next time. Evaluation of actions and changing tack when needed shows flexibility.

You can follow this pattern explicitly and it really helps the recruiter or employer **if you use the words – situation, task, action and result** in your answers in the appropriate sections. They can see where you are and will fill out their notes fully. This is a win/win. It makes their job easy so they can recommend you on for interview.

Don't be concerned if it seems a bit repetitive. The important thing is to give them real information that they can base their decision on. The more real information they have on you, the higher your chances of being selected for the interview. If you are a really good writer, you can mix it up a bit, but ensure that you are giving real and relevant information.

∞